Nurturing Spiritual Depth in Christian Worship

Ten Practices

Janice Jean Springer

RESOURCE PUBLICATIONS, INC.
San Jose, California

© 2009 Resource Publications, Inc. All rights reserved. No part of this book may be photocopied or otherwise reproduced without permission from the publisher. For reprint permission, contact:

Reprint Department
Resource Publications, Inc.
160 E. Virginia Street, Suite #290
San Jose, CA 95112-5876
(408) 286-8505 • (408) 287-8748 fax

Library of Congress Cataloging-in-Publication Data

Springer, Janice Jean, 1945-
    Nurturing spiritual depth in Christian worship : ten practices / Janice Jean Springer.
        p. cm.
    Includes bibliographical references.
    ISBN-13: 978-0-89390-679-5 (pbk.)
    ISBN-10: 0-89390-679-4 (pbk.)
    1. Worship. 2. Spirituality. I. Title.
    BV10.3.S67 2009
    264—dc22

                                        2009006824

Printed in the United States of America
09 10 11 12 13 | 5 4 3 2 1

Design and production: Kenneth Guentert, The Publishing Pro, LLC
Copyeditor: Laura Quilling
Photo of author: Annie Florin, annieflorinphotography.com

Contents

Acknowledgments   iv
Giving Thanks   v
Call to Worship   vii
My Assumptions about Worship   xiii

Practice #1: Lead Worship from a Place of Deep Prayer   1
Practice #2: Consider What Happens to the Energy   12
Practice #3: Move People out of Their Heads   32
Practice #4: Read Scripture So Nobody's Bored   44
Practice #5: Make Every Part Match   56
Practice #6: Use Fewer Words   63
Practice #7: Create a Safe Intimacy   73
Practice #8: Make Worship Inclusive   86
Practice #9: Integrate Music More Fully   104
Practice #10: Insist on Integrity in the Worship Service   118

Benediction   134
Further Reading   137
Notes   140

Acknowledgments

Excerpt from *Radiance: A Spiritual Memoir of Evelyn Underhill*, compiled and edited by Bernard Bangley. © 2004 by Bernard Bangley. Used by permission of Paraclete Press; www.paracletepress.com.

Scripture quotation from *The Message*, © 1993, 1994, 1995, 1996, 2000, 2001, 2002 by Eugene H. Peterson. Used by permission of NavPress Publishing Group.

Excerpts from *From Brokenness to Community*, by Jean Vanier. © 1992 by the President and Fellows of Harvard University. Paulist Press, Inc., New York/Mahwah, NJ. Used by permission of Paulist Press, Inc., www.paulistpress.com.

Scripture quotations from the *New Revised Standard Version Bible*, © 1989 by the Division of Christian Education of the National Council of the Churches of Christ in the U.S.A. Used by permission. All rights reserved.

Giving Thanks

Sometimes I take a set of prayer beads and offer my thanksgivings, naming one blessing as I finger each bead. Giving thanks for those who made it possible for me to write this book keeps my praying fingers busy for a long time.

I begin by giving great thanks for my parents, David and Arlene Springer, models of faithfulness and love. My mother died many years ago and my father while this book was in process, but I continue to lean on their gentle, unfailing love. It is because of them that I have such affection for the church. It is because of them that I have been able to receive God's unconditional love.

I finger many beads as I thank my network of precious family and friends. You listen to my woes and believe in my ministry. You give me tea for comfort and grandchildren for delight. You rescue me from computer problems and sustain me with your love and hugs. For each of you, and especially for my sister, Nancy Raim; for my children and their spouses, David and Cheryl Shannon, Christie and Dave Goodman, and Katy and Paul Simon; and for my best friend Donna Shearman; thanks be to God. I thank all the churches that I have served: St. Paul's United Church of Christ in Defiance, Missouri; Church of Christ United in Winthrop, Iowa; Phoenix Community Church, United Church of Christ in Kalamazoo, Michigan; and University Congregational United Church of Christ in Missoula, Montana. Thank you for letting me love you. You trusted me with your worship traditions, and you taught me how vital it is that worship takes us deeper than the surface of God.

I offer thanks for those friends and colleagues who served as readers for this manuscript: Ken Arthur, Whitney Brown, Fred Cunningham, Jo Cunningham, Debbie Eisenbise, Winnie Ganshaw, Scott Helms, Angie Howse-Willard, Jonna Jensen, Karen Sanborn, Nancy Stroupe, Randy Thomas, Barb Van Eck, Susan Weier, and Aud Wierenga. Your suggestions were wise, and they improved this book. Besides that, each of you encouraged me by insisting that these ideas about worship needed to be shared; I thank you. I also thank Scott Helms for some specific musical insights that guided my work in Practice #9.

Thanks to the good folks at Resource Publications, Inc., who turned my manuscript into a book. Kathi Scarpace offered her careful editing. Caroline Thomas, ministry consultant, not only worked on my behalf, but also sent me encouraging emails. Mary Dent, production coordinator; Laura Quilling, copyeditor; and Ken Guentert, design and production, worked faithfully on details that are not even on my radar screen. I am grateful to all of you. Most of all, I thank Bill Burns, publisher. Bill, I appreciate your humor, your expansive, ecumenical vision, and your willingness to take a chance. Thank you.

My fingers move through the beads, and I give thanks for Susan Weier. For your appreciation of my worship leadership, for your support and encouragement, for your faith in my ministry and your belief in this book, for shared prayers and shared promises, I give you my love and gratitude. Thanks be to God for you.

And finally, I offer great thanks to the people of Phoenix Community Church, United Church of Christ, of Kalamazoo, Michigan, whom I served for eleven years. Your creativity, your openness, your honesty, your pain, and your rejoicing were the catalyst for most of this work. I am grateful for our ministry together, and I thank you with all my heart. If this book helps deepen the worship of other congregations, it is because of you. With love and gratitude, I dedicate this book to you.

Call to Worship

Yet like many folks, I often feel that when it comes to church, I am standing in a river, dying of thirst.

—*Jan L. Richardson*[1]

Some years ago I faced a very challenging parish ministry. The church was small, young, and not yet quite stable. Many of its members had been badly wounded by their experiences of the Christian tradition and were hostile to it. Others felt they had outgrown the Christian story and were apathetic toward it. Many people in the congregation—women, lesbians and gays, folks with disabilities, the poor—had been marginalized by family, by society, or by previous churches; wary, they did not give authority to pastor, tradition, scripture, or Jesus. They had access to every faith path in the world, ancient and new, and valued creating their own spirituality, seeing no need for the Christian tradition. I was overwhelmed with the challenges this community offered me.

Desperate, I prayed, "Show me what to do, Lord." It seemed to me that the answer came in a vision: I saw magnificent whales rising above the water, then diving deep into the ocean, and I heard these words: *Take them to the depths where the whales are.*

I served—and loved—that church for eleven good years, and that vision shaped all of my ministry: *Take them to the depths where the whales are.* In Christian education, in spiritual direction, in community-building, in mission and justice work, and most especially in worship, I tried to take not only the congregation but also myself as pastor into the depths: the depths of the issues, the depths of our Christian faith, the depths of ourselves, the depths of God. And there was abundant new life.

"Going into the depth" is a metaphor for going to the center, to the essence, to the source. It's about moving beyond the surface and the superficial and moving to the core of truth. Experiencing life (or faith or prayer or God or worship) from a place of depth moves us out of our ordinary perceptions. Our view of reality changes; new possibilities emerge. A depth experience takes us beyond our defenses. It opens our hearts and minds. Healing happens.

Our language about God is not God; our concepts of God are not God. They are only imperfect symbols of the Mystery beyond language and concepts. Faith that comes from the depth brings us closer to a lived experience of the Holy One who is beyond all images. That's when we move into the new life to which Jesus calls us.

For many years I have been gripped by a passion to plan, lead, and experience worship that offers a doorway into those depth places. When I am able to do so, people find worship to be compelling; they respond with an amazing gratitude. It is as if I just offered food to people who have been hungry for a very long time. My skill as worship leader is not what satisfies their hunger. They are fed when worship takes them into the deep places where they encounter their true selves and the living God.

Why doesn't that happen more often in Christian worship? That is certainly the intent of all worship leaders: to help people connect with God. Yet for more and more of us, there is a growing disconnect between our worship and our lives. Is that why so many leave our churches? Why are we turning to other faith traditions to learn how to meditate, to find spiritual practices that move us beyond the surface of life? Why has no one taught us the same resources from our own tradition? Why do so many of us leave worship comforted perhaps but not changed?

I am greatly disheartened by the worship I experience in many Christian churches. During too many worship services, I feel like we are standing on a whale fishing for minnows. We talk about the God who pulls off resurrection, yet our worship is anemic. We proclaim the good news, yet the worshipers look like they haven't heard any for a long time. We speak of the God who empowers us, yet the energy of the worship hour is flat, even draining. We pride ourselves on inclusion, yet we structure worship in such a way that many are excluded. We call ourselves disciples, yet we worship like consumers. We hear about the radical way of Jesus, yet worship reflects little visible difference between the culture and the faith community. We claim to be there to worship God, yet our worship service is mostly about us. The god of many churches is too small to be of much use, and worship reflects that.

This book explores what worship can look like if it comes from a place of depth. I talk about how to design and lead worship that has the capacity for leading not only the people but also the worship leader into that depth: worship that honors our heads (our thinking selves) but moves us beyond our heads to our hearts (our feelings and relational selves) and even deeper to our souls (where we encounter God and our true selves).

I offer tools to pastors and lay leaders that will allow them to deepen their congregation's worship so hungry people will more often get fed; so worshipers will not just learn about God, but will also experience God; so people who know in their heart of hearts that they are not loving enough can change; and so those who care about this world can be partners in its healing.

I have led worship in both progressive and traditional churches, in young churches and seasoned ones, in rural communities and in cities. In some places, I was a long-term called pastor; in others, a guest for one Sunday. The tools in this book, used to deepen the worship and invite the worshipers deeper, brought forth in each setting responses such as:

- Worship opened my heart today.

- Communion had no meaning for me; today for the first time in years, I came to the table.

- For forty years, I have sat in this choir loft facing the congregation, and I have never once seen them engaged like they were this morning.

- I really heard that scripture for the first time, and it spoke to my soul.

- You won't remember us, but we worshiped at your church once about eight years ago. We still remember the details of that service. Now I am a pastor, and that single worship experience has influenced my ministry.

- Worship here is not a picture to look at but a window to look through to God.

- I had turned my back on the church. Attending worship [here] opened my eyes to what church could and should be ... and helped to bring me into a fuller and richer relationship with the Divine.

- The words of scripture mean something to me now.

- [This worship] gave Jesus back to me.

These responses—actual quotes from congregants in various churches—indicate to me that these worship services engage people in new ways; the services open them and deepen their faith. It is not a nice sermon or a pretty anthem that does it—the whole worship experience takes people deeper into their own struggles and, most of all, deeper into the presence and power of God. There hungry people find food.

The resources in this book do not require that you adopt some new style of worship or change the hymns you sing. You do not have to give up your organ and buy drums—or give up your drums and buy an organ. Deep worship can happen in any church, whatever its worship tradition. I have had my closed heart opened in a Catholic Mass and in Quaker silence, in a small rural congregation and in a massive French cathedral; I've experienced my soul awakening while singing "Rock of Ages" and while singing "Siyhamba." I want to show you how to use the worship practices that you already value to invite and empower your congregation to move more deeply into God. The tools I offer can help you make worship more vital, more authentic, more vibrant, and more God-centered. That will happen if the worship leader and the worship come out of the depth of Spirit.

I made this book practical and accessible. Each chapter offers one tool that can deepen and strengthen your worship and many concrete applications of that tool. You might think of these tools as spiritual practices for worship leaders. This book is for pastors, of course, but also for anyone who offers leadership in worship, as laypeople often do; I have taught these ideas to laity as well as to clergy. The book will be useful to worship committees that help shape the worship traditions of their churches, and it also lends itself to being the catalyst for group discussion—with pastor and people both involved—when a community is looking at its worship life. Sometimes deep worship happens because of the pastor's commitment, and sometimes it happens because the people demand it.

I have a great passion for worship. I love to plan it, to lead it, to experience it. I've been in the church all my life, and I have served as pastor for twenty-eight years, planning and leading worship in four very different churches (and as an interim sabbatical pastor or guest pastor in many others). Out of that experience, out of the comments that laypeople and colleagues have made to me, and out of my own hunger for the depth of faith, I have written this book.

The examples I use come from churches I've served and churches

I've visited. I've been in the pulpit, and I've been in the pew; and both perspectives have taught me a lot about worship. I've learned much from watching other pastors who lead powerful worship, and I've learned from observing worship in which people are obviously bored. I've learned from parishioners who cared enough about worship to challenge me, and I've learned from my own mistakes.

I believe that worship should feed us. I also believe that it should transform us. Just helping me get through another week is not enough for me. I want to be transformed. I want to be made into a new being. It may happen slowly (usually does); it may happen in undramatic ways (almost always). But worship should change the way we look at the world. It should alter what we value. It should rearrange our allegiances. It should reduce our ego from master to servant. It should make the most timid of us find courage. It should turn us into disciples of Jesus the Christ. Transformation: That's what I expect of worship. That's what I believe is possible.

Take them to the depths where the whales are. May this book help you design and lead worship that will guide not only the congregation but also you, the worship leader, into the depths: the depths of our Christian faith, the depths of our hearts and souls, the depths of community, the depths of prayer, the depths of God.

My Assumptions about Worship

Our primary mission is not to help change the world, but to be the church: to be a community that worships the God of Jesus amidst a culture that worships other gods.

—*Martin B. Copenhaver, Anthony B. Robinson, and William H. Willimon*[1]

I want to name the assumptions I make about what is true and necessary in Christian worship, because if you are considering my ideas about worship, you have a right to know where I am coming from. I hope these thoughts will challenge you to ponder your own assumptions. I hope that you will discuss them in an adult education class, at a church retreat, in a worship committee meeting. I suppose, in a very simple form, the following is my theology of worship:

- *Worship is the central act of the faith community.*

- *Worship is first and foremost about recognizing as Ultimate Reality the Great Mystery that we name God. That makes worship different from a pep rally or a talk show or a concert or a support group session. Worship should center on the power of God more than on the problems of people. Worship includes praise, adoration, thanksgiving. Worship is about being in relationship with Ultimate Reality. In worship, we are able to know about God. In really good worship, we can be led to know God.*

■ *Worship grows out of our scripture: its words, its stories, its truths.*

■ *Christian worship flows from Christ. Though worship may be either Christocentric or theocentric, and though some regard Jesus as Lord and Savior and some know him simply as* teacher, *the way of Christ is always foundational.*

■ *The Easter message should be central in every service: the message of hope, of transformation, of new life, of God's power to bring life out of death.*

■ *Worship should create disciples, people who commit themselves to the way of prayer, compassion, and justice that Jesus taught and modeled.*

■ *Good worship is always political (which is not the same as talking about politics). It is always countercultural. It is always protest. Worship is a community's most radical political act.*

■ *Worship is the church's unique contribution to the struggle for justice in the world.[2] Worship will include issues of justice and global perspectives, but it cannot be reduced to an activist rally.*

■ *Worship should welcome all people; in that way, it models the radically inclusive love of God and the community-building way of Jesus.*

■ *Worship is a communal act, as Christianity is a communal faith.*

■ *The people in worship are a congregation, not an audience. They come as community, not as consumers.*

■ *Worship should speak to the whole person: body, mind, heart, soul. Worship should have enough variety (not in every service, but over time) to appeal to diverse personalities.*

■ *There is no one right way to worship. The diversity of worship in the Christian tradition is one of our gifts and strengths.*

■ *Christianity stands alongside the other world spiritual traditions as the carriers of our species' best wisdom and deepest truths. We are not in competition with other faiths. Some of our best truths are universal, found in all major religions. Some of our best truths are unique, our particular gift to the human journey. We do well to learn from other traditions, but the goal of that learning is always to go deeper into our own tradition.*

Now let's begin our exploration of how we might deepen Christian worship.

Lead Worship from a Place of Deep Prayer

Sometimes we worship leaders are in such a hurry to transmit that we forget that our primary duty is to receive.
—*Evelyn Underhill*[1]

For several years, I dreamed of teaching classes for clergy and lay folks about worship: how to design and lead worship so it moves us beyond our heads and into our hearts and souls, so it takes us into the depths of ourselves and the depths of God. I was talking with some colleagues once who asked what I would teach if I had such an opportunity. I quickly named some topics and then stopped. I was silent for a moment, and then I said, "For half the class, I would teach about worship. The other half of the class would be about deep prayer."

I am convinced that the most important human ingredient of faithful worship is the prayer life of the pastor or worship leader. This chapter explores that statement. I made this the beginning place because everything else in this book grows out of what is written here.

In our postmodern world, the church faces the challenge of safeguarding the role of pastor. Religious institutions break down; religious leaders are not granted the authority we once knew. As people become familiar with a variety of helping professionals, we pastors are pressured to become one of those. We are seen as CEOs or as therapists or as social workers or as political activists. Often we ourselves are more comfortable with one of these models than with the nebulous role of *pastor*. The demands of our particular ministry setting or the expectations of our parishioners frequently seem to force these roles on us.

Pastors do wear many hats, and our tasks sometimes overlap with those of other helping professionals. We *are* teachers and administrators and counselors. But what we really are—and what we are called to be—is spiritual leaders. That is our primary role. Our most important function as pastor or priest is to act as a channel for Spirit so Spirit can manifest in human consciousness and to bless—empower—our people to be such channels also.[2] That is what our congregations need from us. They can find competent administrators and caring therapists, better trained in their fields than we are, in other places. What our churches need is spiritual leadership, and to be spiritual leaders, we must be people of deep prayer.

All pastors pray. But most of us know the struggle to maintain a practice of deep prayer when the demands of ministry (not to mention family, household, and self-care) are so overwhelming. Too often our prayer life happens as we are driving in the car to the next hospital visit. It may not be all we want, but it feels like the best we can manage.

Lay leaders may not have the same struggle about their role as pastors, but they do have the same struggle with time. Our culture moves at warp speed, and all of us are overwhelmed with more demands and more delights than we can possibly hold together. Somehow in the midst of it all, we are supposed to find time for a spiritual practice too!

A prayer life that is squeezed into the spare moments here and there is not necessarily lacking in sincerity or authenticity. It is a good way to pray. But by itself, it is not a practice of deep prayer.

Deep Prayer

Deep prayer happens when we get out of our heads, when we move beyond words and concepts and thinking. It happens when we go beyond talking (even to God) and move into listening. It happens when we make friends with stillness. It happens when we let go. Deep prayer requires focus. It requires discipline. It requires commitment. That means it requires time.

The classic mode of deep prayer is sitting in silence and stilling (at least to some degree) the mind. The modern practices of Centering Prayer and Christian Meditation each offer us simple techniques for doing that, for quieting our minds and welcoming silence. The Jesus Prayer (repetition of the phrase "Lord Jesus Christ, Son of God, have mercy on me") can lead us into the depths of prayer. Saying the Rosary and praying with prayer beads are other forms of prayer that can lead us into a contemplative space beyond ego and beyond conceptual thinking. Breath prayer (which involves slowing and deepening our breathing) can do this. *Lectio Divina* is reading a short portion of scripture and meditating on just one word or phrase; that practice can lead us into deep prayer. The practice of present moment awareness, or mindfulness, can lead us to a place of depth. Let's consider why such prayer practices are so important.

Leading worship is heady stuff. It can be a position of great power, and a danger is that the worship leader's ego gets in the way of worship. There is no guarantee against this, but a faithful practice of deep prayer is a good precaution. Deep prayer is not about the person praying: It is about God. By its nature, it moves one beyond ego, and thus may help the worship leader to avoid the temptation to use worship to showcase his own gifts or her own life story. If I am faithful to a daily practice of deep prayer, I am more likely to recognize when I am using worship to fill my unconscious desire for attention or affirmation or control.

Deep prayer puts a check on one's ego. It also helps us to grow into the challenging truth that the ego is not really who we are. Ego is the self that we usually think of as *me*. It is the part of us that sees ourselves as separate from other beings and always defends this separate identity. It is the false self, the self instead of the Self. Theologian Beatrice Bruteau describes ego as the descriptions we have of ourselves:[3] woman, runner, Asian-American, activist, organic farmer, Cardinals fan, survivor, even-tempered, smart, compassionate, impatient, and so on. But we are something deeper than our descriptions. All of the world's major religious traditions teach us that we must move beyond ego, beyond the consciousness that insists on defending the small self, the false self, one's separate identity. Moving beyond the ego does not mean eliminating it, but rather, as Episcopal priest Cynthia Bourgeault writes, "displacing it as the seat of one's personal identity. The process is rather like discovering that the earth revolves around the sun rather than vice versa."[4] Only when we can do that are we open to knowing the reality of God (as much as we can know it) instead of just the images of God. Only when we can move beyond the ego self can we fully live out of the compassion that so characterized Jesus. And this is the vital point: Only when we ourselves know that we are more than our small selves can we hope to foster this awareness in our people. Deep prayer is the classic tool for this process.

There is another reason worship leaders need to live out of a deep place of Spirit. Good worship leadership requires that we be attentive to what is happening to the congregation throughout the service. We would hope to be sensitive enough to tell when we are losing the people, when we are threatening them, when we have opened their hearts. Each awareness might demand a particular response, even in the midst of a worship service. Knowledge of such attitudes in the worshiping congregation will certainly influence us as we design worship. What holds the people's attention? What opens their hearts? What makes their eyes glaze over? What causes them to forget all about looking at their watches? What keeps them thinking about their to-do list? What allows the truths of Jesus to pierce their souls? We learn the answers to these questions by learning to be fully awake and aware in the present moment. This is called mindfulness, or present moment awareness, and it is an ancient spiritual practice, one that is fostered in deep prayer in which we learn to live not in the past or the future, but fully in the present moment. Jesus was a master of this: He was fully present to whatever or whoever was in front of him in the moment, and that gave him a calm centeredness and a profound compassion. This is the context out of which sensitive worship leadership can grow.

Let's review before we move on. Why is the practice of deep prayer vital for the pastor or worship leader? It makes it less likely that the pastor's own ego needs will get in the way of worship. It allows the pastor to experience, and therefore help his people experience, that we are something deeper than the descriptions of ourselves. It enables the worship leader to be aware of the feelings and needs of her congregation in the present moment. Deep prayer also allows us to encounter the God beyond all names and images, the God beyond language and concepts. This is where we experience new life, where we find transformation. This is the Source. If the worship leader has not touched this deep place, how can he invite others there?

While our culture is quite disenchanted with organized religion, it is very excited about spirituality. We are used to hearing about yoga and meditation and breath work. We are encouraged to adopt these practices to handle stress or lower our blood pressure or strengthen our immune system. But as people of faith, we move into deep silence or contemplative prayer primarily for another reason. We believe that we are in relationship with the One Who is the Source of all, the Ultimate Reality. We sit in prayer not because of any benefits that come to us, though these are welcome, but because of that relationship with our Source. God is our Beloved, and in prayer we are making love. Our lovemaking might begin with words—our thanksgivings, our petitions, our praise. But our love ultimately takes us beyond words and into Mystery, and in that deep place beyond words, what we experience and practice is silence. It is out of this silence that good ministry happens. It is out of this silence that profound worship emerges.

Qualities Nurtured by Deep Prayer

There are some qualities associated with deep prayer, with the silence beyond conceptual thinking. As our prayer life becomes deeper, we grow into these characteristics, however imperfectly. Our life gradually reshapes itself to integrate these qualities. When this happens, we can design and lead worship capable of inviting our people into their own deep places of encounter and healing.

One caution: Read these qualities gently. They are not goals we must achieve. They are descriptors of a state of consciousness toward which (slowly, over a lifetime) we will grow. They are signposts pointing a direction; that's all. Striving to achieve even these vital qualities is a contradiction of all that the contemplative life is about. This is God's to-do list, not ours. All we have to do is offer God the time, the quiet, and the permission to go to it. God does this work while we rest in the stillness.

How Our Lives Might Look
When They Emerge from Deep Prayer

- We experience God directly (at least in a limited way) so that we know God rather than just knowing about God.

- We understand God both as form (Father, Beloved, Divine Mother) and as beyond form (Mystery beyond all words, concepts, and images).

- We live in or toward union with God, a union that takes us beyond dualism.

- We recognize in ourselves the indwelling Christ.

- We are centered.

- We are less ego-driven.

- We live more in the present moment than in the past or future.

- We experience healing in ourselves where it is needed.

- We live more out of trust than fear.

- We know ourselves to be loved and accepted; we love and accept ourselves.

- We have an ever-deepening capacity to love.

- We become more sensitive to the suffering and needs of others.

- We have more clarity about what is important and what is not.

- We are open to the source of creativity, and so our work, our thinking, and our problem-solving become more creative.

- We are less interested in defending (our ego, our status, our rights) and more interested in serving.

- We claim a model of reality, a paradigm, different from the model our culture upholds. Because of this, we perceive everything differently.

- We recognize the oneness of all creation, not as metaphor or vision but as reality.

- We experience a knowing that is deeper than our intellectual knowing, and we find it is trustworthy.

When these changes happen, however imperfectly, we begin to move into a different state of consciousness, what we might call Christ consciousness, perhaps similar to what our Buddhist neighbors might refer to as the Buddha nature. I believe that it is from this place that profound worship evolves.

Making Time

Of course, we are all in favor of spiritual practices that will lead us to the place to which this list of qualities points. But in our high-speed culture and high-demand lives, just thinking about finding time for a set-apart prayer period can overwhelm us. It feels like one more demand. So before we move on to talk more specifically about worship, let me address two parts of this issue: finding time for prayer and living prayerfully outside of a set-apart prayer period.

There are many books about deep prayer (some are listed in Further Reading), and they all address the struggle we have to keep the discipline, to find the time. I encourage you to look at those books or talk to others who manage to make time for silence and stillness. Bourgeault's blunt words are vital: "Virtually every spiritual tradition that holds a vision of human transformation at its heart also claims that a practice of intentional silence is non-negotiable. Period. You just have to do it."[5] I will get you started by sharing a few things that work for me.

- I try to remain flexible. My prayer time has been different at different times in my life. Now I have the delight of two extended prayer periods each day. When I had small children, that was not possible for me.

- I have found, as most teachers will suggest, that morning is my best prayer time, first thing, before the demands of the day overwhelm me, before my "monkey mind"—which leaps incessantly from one thought to the next—is up to full speed.

■ I write prayer time on my calendar like an appointment and honor it like I would any appointment (it is, after all, an appointment with God and my deepest self). If I don't do that, it doesn't happen. Sometimes I have to say no to some good opportunities because I already have a commitment: my time set apart for meditation.

■ Because I take this appointment as seriously as I would any vital meeting, I turn off my phone, put out the cat, tell my family or staff I am not to be disturbed.

I've found that I need to be creative in making time for such prayer, and though I can't always make all the time I'd like, I can almost always make some time, so I begin there. I've learned two things: Any discipline gets difficult at times, and my mind is very gifted at finding really good reasons why I should give up my prayer practice. But I don't. Worship leadership is not the reason I sit in silent prayer every day, but it is true that after decades of such prayer, I can no longer imagine leading worship outside of this practice.

Living Contemplatively

Whether or not you set apart time for a deep prayer practice, in the course of your day you can find ways to live more contemplatively and nurture this new consciousness. In fact, when you care for small children or a loved one who is ill, your primary prayer practice may be your daily life and the service it entails. The following suggestions might help you, in the course of your daily routines, open into the deep places of your soul and your faith:

■ *Cultivate silence.* If you have five minutes alone in the car, maybe the silence will be more useful to you than the evening news on the car radio. Do you really need your iPod with you on every walk?

- *Fast from the news.* Limit how much you read the paper, how long you sit in front of the TV. These sources feed you hopelessness and despair along with the news.

- *Read alternative sources.* Find sources that do not operate from the culture's paradigm. Read periodicals devoted to justice, peace, and nonviolence. Read novels written by marginalized people. Read about quantum physics. Read the great mystics of our faith. Read perspectives from other world religions, other ethnic groups, other cultures.

- *Practice breath work.* Learn to breathe deeply. Practice simple deep breathing before your prayer. Discover that you can't breathe slowly and deeply and be angry at the same time.

- *Slow down.* Live free of clocks once in awhile. Say no to more opportunities, even good ones. Be content with fewer options.

- *Connect with other species and life-forms.* Begin with your family pet. Walk in the woods. Sit at the seashore. Don't walk past the daffodils without pausing to really look at them. Consider what effect your life and your choices have on the earth and the other life-forms that live on it with you. Stop long enough to be awed by the sunset, the snowfall.

- *Live in beauty.* Music, art, gardens—whatever moves you with deep beauty—fill your life with it. Don't mistake true beauty for its imitators: luxury, abundance, affluence, popularity.

- *Look at life through the eyes of the other.* This profound spiritual discipline will open your heart and tame your ego. Some days you can look at life through the eyes of your beloved—some days. Keep at it until you can see through the eyes of your enemy.

- *Practice mindfulness.* Be in the present moment. Focus on what is right before you. Notice how often your mind is on the past or the future. Notice how often the present moment is free of pain. Keep coming back to present moment awareness.

■ *Keep Sabbath.* Set aside time for silence, solitude, and slowness; time to rest, renew, and refocus; time just to be with God. Daily prayer, weekly time off from work obligations, a monthly or quarterly day of quiet, annual week-long retreats, sabbaticals every five to seven years: Begin where you can and work toward more. Resist the constant temptation to give this time away, to allow obligations to intrude.

■ *Practice compassion and forgiveness.* Practice it some more. Make a practice of it. Make it a practice.

I hope you read these ideas gently too. They are not goals you must achieve in order to find God, in order to be worthy. Rather, they are ways of being in the world that will feed your deepest, hungriest places. These ways of being, like more formal contemplative prayer, can lead you into the depths, the place of transformation. When that begins to happen to you, it will also happen to the worship you design or lead, and when it happens to the worship, it will happen to the worshipers who want so much to be fed.

And now, in the context of this deep prayer and soulful living, let's turn to worship.

Practice #2

Consider What Happens to the Energy

**Spirituality is more than belief.
It is a potent conductor of energy.**
—*Judith Orloff*[1]

Worship can be—I would say it *should* be—about power. It is about God's power. It is about how we can access that power for our lives, for our service to others, for our justice-making. It is about how not to abuse power. Because power is energy, I have learned to pay attention to energy in worship. I notice that if I fail to do so, most of us will not get out of our heads, will not bond with the community, and will not be empowered. If I, as worship leader, do not pay attention to the energy, most of us will not feel that we have touched—or been touched by—the Sacred.

You may be aware of the words *prana, chi,* and *biofields.* These terms are not always interchangeable; they each have specific meanings in their traditions or fields, but at the very least, they each refer to energy, to what we might call the life force. *Prana* comes from the Hindu tradition; perhaps you have heard it in yoga practice or meditation class. *Chi* is Chinese, as in the practice of tai chi. The term *biofields,* or energy fields, is contemporary scientific language. From these different traditions, each word acknowledges the energy that is the life force within us. In our tradition, some would say we are referring to that life force when we talk of the Holy Spirit.

We are not talking about energy in the sense of vitality, whether one is perky or sluggish, eager or depressed, though there is some relationship between those feelings and the life force. We are talking about the force of life within creation, the power of God, the presence of the Holy Mystery that brings and sustains life. We are not in control of this life force, but when we practice yoga or tai chi or meditation or deep breathing, we do learn to access it, to channel it, to increase it. Worship can offer the same opportunity. Worship either helps us access *prana* for our lives or fails to. Worship enables us to be filled with Spirit, empowered for love and service, or it leaves us feeling empty, weak, and depleted. Worship shows us how to build and strengthen the *chi* in our lives, or it has no effect on whether we feel weary and powerless.

Of all the things I have taught about worship, the subject of energy in worship generates, from clergy and laypeople alike, the most excitement and the most requests for more. But it is not an easy subject to discuss. Like all mystery, it is an experience bigger than our language can contain or, therefore, describe. Even the word *energy* is nebulous: What exactly are we talking about? (The answer to that is, no one knows.) Are we talking about ever-changing human emotions, or are we talking about the movement of God? Are we making room for Spirit to work, or are we just manipulating people?

Moreover, very little has been written about *prana* in worship. Intensive study of energy, a trustworthy intuition, and decades of experience leading worship have led me to this place, and I invite you to explore it with me, realizing that we are just exploring and will not offer the last word on the subject. We are looking into a new way to understand worship, a way to help us perceive what is really happening in worship (whether we perceive it or not, it is still happening).

Let me tell you how I will proceed. First I will try to help you understand what I mean when I talk about energy in worship. We'll look at several ways of designing parts of a worship service to see how each design affects the *prana* in the sanctuary and in the people. Then I will talk about some of the energetic tasks that fall to the worship leader. This may give you some new ways, more expansive ways, of understanding the role of the pastor or other worship leader. I will end by responding to some of the questions and concerns that people have addressed to me in relation to this work. Let's begin by trying to understand this life force, *prana,* in the context of a worship service.

Understanding Energy in Worship

Though it may seem strange, perhaps even uncomfortable, to talk about something that is as hard to pin down as energy—and to use foreign words at that—you already have much experience working with *chi* in worship. Imagine yourself standing in front of your congregation; maybe it will be easiest if you think of a particular, significant incident. Perhaps you remember the first time you served as a lay reader and how nervous you were. Perhaps you were in front of your people as pastor, having just announced that you and your spouse were expecting your first baby. Perhaps you welcomed the community to worship in the school gym the first Sunday after your church burned. Perhaps you called out "Christ is risen!" to your people on Easter Sunday morning. Choose such an incident and remember it. What did you feel? What came at you? Did you feel the congregation's expectancy? Excitement? Anxiety? Before you began to talk, did you feel their boredom or restlessness? Did you feel their support for you? Was the community in shock or grief? Were they bonded together, as can happen after some crises, or estranged and hostile, as can happen after other kinds of crises? Did you feel that the congregation was with you? Or were they scattered and unfocused?

If you were able to sense any of these things, you have already experienced reading the *prana,* the energy, in a people or in a space. If you did anything in response to that energy (named it, gained strength from it, braced yourself to face it, made the congregation aware of it), you were working with *prana* in worship.

Think about the difference between a Good Friday service and an Easter morning service. The mood is obviously very different. The hymns are different, the scripture is different, and the energy is also different. As worship planner (with a lot of help from tradition), you planned that difference into the service. You wanted and expected one mood on Good Friday and quite another on Easter. You worked with *prana* in worship.

We can learn about this life energy in many different places. The esoteric and mystical corners of our Christian tradition know a lot about it, as do similar sources in other world religions. We learn about *prana* by studying yoga or the martial arts. The most progressive voices in physics and biology today are full of discussions about energy. Energy medicine, once the property of alternative healing fields, is now found not only in Chinese medicine, pranic healing, and biofeedback, but also in more traditional Western medicine. We experience this life energy if we receive or offer healing prayer or the laying on of hands.

From these sources, we learn that some things strengthen our energy, heal it, or increase it. It's not just our momentary vitality that increases; we actually learn how to strengthen the life force that impels our whole being. We learn the correct way to do a yoga posture; we learn to breathe more deeply than usual; we learn that chanting has a different effect on us than jazz; we learn to get off the couch and go walking.

In fact, we can make a list of things that bring positive energy to us, open us to God's healing energy, increase our own *prana*, or strengthen the energy of a group. The following are just a few with which most energy workers would agree. Notice how many of them are part of our religious practices and our worship rituals. These are known to increase the life force, the pranic energy: water, deep slow breathing, silence, prayer, chanting, love, being around another person with good energy. For most Christian traditions, communion is the most sacred channel through which we receive Spirit, the new life of Christ. Each of these things (and many others) have been recognized for centuries as bringing Spirit to us, opening us to healthy, healing energy.

Likewise, some things drain us of *prana*, depleting the life force within us. Some things encourage the presence of negative energy. From your own experience and common sense, you could name many of the items on this list. Notice how many of the following are things people of faith typically (we might say intuitively) speak, write, preach, or teach against, encouraging us to limit, heal, or avoid them. Experiences that are understood to deplete our *prana* include, among others, stress, rushing, multitasking, negativity (bitterness, anger, worry, and so on), hard liquor, shopping malls, television, and dwelling on the past or the future.

If we can accept that some things increase our energy and some things deplete it, that some things strengthen the life force within us and some things weaken it, then it is not hard to take the next step and ask what happens to *prana* in worship. What happens in our worship services that increases and strengthens the life force within us? What happens in our worship that depletes and weakens the energy of the people and of the community? If the life force is somehow connected to God—as surely it is—then what things in worship bring more of Spirit to our people? What things channel more of God's grace and power?

Since the beginning of time, those charged with the care of the spiritual lives of their people—pastors and priests, shamans and medicine women, gurus and imams and rabbis and Zen masters, and desert fathers and mothers—learned how to help people open themselves to more of God's power and life force. They came to understand that some music did it and some did not; that some rituals increased the life force in their people and some did not. They learned that some prohibitions and some practices protected their people from depleted energy (or negative energies). Their understanding about energy may have been quite intuitive or gleaned from centuries of experience, but they learned it.

In our time, we do not take such insights seriously. We evaluate the traditions and words and rituals of Christian worship using only our heads, our thinking selves, that part of us that is most shaped by our culture's model of reality and most controlled by our culture's limitations. Many worship leaders know intuitively what increases or decreases *chi* in our worship, what increases the possibility of worshipers being open to Spirit. They planned and led worship accordingly, even though they may never have articulated their work in terms of *energy*. But others lost such knowledge as their education stressed the rational evaluation of worship, the political more than the spiritual definition of *power*. Perhaps this is one reason why much of our worship has lost its power for people: We no longer come to worship expecting to be changed or healed; we come expecting to be soothed perhaps, but not healed. When we substitute human understandings for the power and presence of God, our worship becomes anemic, and we stop expecting anything more.

Seeing Energy in Worship

It is easier to feel the movement of energy than it is to discuss it, so to help you get a sense of how *prana* moves in worship—and how we can work with it instead of against it—let me give you some examples. As you read them, remember that in a service that opens us to this life force, people leave feeling subtly or dramatically stronger, more openhearted, more at peace, more centered. They feel healed or connected (to self, to community, to God) or compassionate or joyful: All of these feelings are signs of the healing touch of God.

The following examples will be most helpful to you if you read them slowly and reflect on each experience. Imagine that it is the late-night Christmas Eve service at your church. The clock is almost at midnight; with its festive poinsettias and moving solos and life-giving gospel, the service is almost over. It is time to end worship with "Silent Night." I invite you to imagine three churches in the same town, each

at this same moment in the service. All of them are ending the service with "Silent Night," but each handles it in a different way. In your
mind's eye, be present at each of these services (you are able to bilo-
cate, aren't you?), and try to be aware of how the energy in each sanctuary feels. Remember, it's almost midnight, the service in each
church has been beautiful and meaningful, and each congregation is
about to end the service with "Silent Night."

At First Church, the congregation remains seated, the lights are
on, and a gifted soloist sings a moving rendition of "Silent Night"
accompanied by the fine organ. Imagine yourself in that sanctuary.
What do you feel? Can you sense—could you put words to—the energy in the room? What is the feeling in the church as people leave the
sanctuary?

Across the street at Second Church, the congregation stands,
each person holding an unlit candle. The lights are turned out, the
organ begins the music, and in darkness, the congregation begins
singing "Silent Night" as they pass the light of Christ from one person
to another, one candle to another. There is no light at first, but none
is needed; everyone knows verse one by heart. The worshipers watch
the dark sanctuary slowly fill with a soft glow as they light more and
more candles. The modest light enables the congregation to read the
printed words of later verses; the people follow the lead of the organ
in their singing. Can you imagine this service? What do you feel? Can
you sense—can you describe—the energy in the sanctuary during this
part of the service? What is the feeling in the church as the service
comes to an end?

Around the block at Third Church, the experience is much the
same as at Second Church—darkness and candles, people standing
and singing—but with one difference: The congregation sings a cappella. The organ helps them start but drops out after a phrase or two,
and it is just the voice of the people singing in the darkness, darkness
that is slowly becoming filled with light. What do you feel? Can you
sense—are you able to talk about—the energy in the sanctuary dur-

ing "Silent Night"? What is the feeling in the church as the people prepare to leave?

If you felt a difference between those three ways of ending the Christmas Eve service (whether or not you can articulate it well), then you are able to read the energy, to observe the movement of *prana* in a worship service. Perhaps you're beginning to understand that the way we plan worship affects the type of energy that surrounds our people and the weakness or strength of the *chi* with which we send them home.

Let me tell you my experiences with these three church services. My purpose is not to say that there is only one right way to sing "Silent Night," but rather to use a familiar example to show what happens to the *prana*. Of course, it happens whether we acknowledge it or not.

First Church left the lights on, which communicates business as usual. At Second and Third Churches, the darkness not only symbolizes the darkness from which Christ comes to deliver us, but it also says, "Something special is happening. Business as usual is suspended. Pay attention." The experience of darkness helps to build the energy because of the expectation, because the beauty opens people's hearts, because the darkness eliminates distractions, and because the candlelight and the candle lighting focus attention.

At First Church, the congregation was in the role of audience. Energy is generally lower for an observer than for a participant. Listening to a solo is a wonderful part of worship, but it may not be the best way to end such a powerful service. A moving solo certainly increases *prana*, but with a carol as beloved as this one, with all its associations and memories, participation strengthens *prana* much more. There is also less energy when the congregation is sitting instead of standing.

Second Church and Third Church, but not First, chose to do the traditional candle lighting during the singing. This holding and passing of the light in the darkness—this experiential acting out of the coming of Christ—is very powerful and raises the level of *prana* considerably.

Second and Third Churches designed the ending of the service the same way except for one difference: At Third Church, the congregation sang a cappella. Could you feel any difference when you imagined singing with the organ at Second Church and singing a cappella at Third? The organ (or the piano or guitar or keyboard or band) is beautiful and allows people to sing more confidently, freed a bit of their self-consciousness. And singing a cappella can be risky if the congregation loses the tune or gets slower with each verse. But assuming the congregation has a little ability to do this (they don't need to be perfect), singing a cappella witnesses to our vulnerability but also to our courage, and that is very moving. The quietness, especially coupled with the darkness, slows our minds, and that is very healing. Singing a cappella, particularly in a congregation that doesn't do it very often, enables us to realize (not necessarily at a conscious level) that we are not just individuals but a fragile, yet capable, community, and to make it, we need one another. That is very empowering.

At Third Church, the *prana* was quieter, but much stronger and much deeper. I suspect that more people left that service feeling fed, feeling blessed, feeling touched by love, than did their neighbors at First and Second. I would guess that more people moved out of their heads and into their hearts or souls at Third Church; while at Second and even more so at First, more people stayed in their heads, their thinking selves.

Here is another example. Once again, I invite you to imagine the difference in the life force you feel, the energy, the spirit in yourself and in the congregation: It is Easter morning. Smell the lilies, see the bright colors in the clothes and the banners, feel the festivity in the air.

At the United Church on the Hill, the congregation sits while someone reads the gospel story of the empty tomb; let's assume that it is read very well, with appropriate feeling and eye contact. The reading ends, there is a pause of about five seconds, the pianist plays a full verse introduction, and then while remaining seated, the congregation sings a rousing Caribbean "Hallelujah," which about half of the congregation knows. What might that be like for you?

Meanwhile, at the United Church in the Valley, the congregation stands, the worship leader speaks the gospel from memory (and does it very well, with appropriate feeling and eye contact). No sooner is the last word spoken than the pianist, with only one brief chord as introduction, immediately leads the congregation into a rousing Caribbean "Hallelujah," which nearly all of that congregation knows very well. What might this feel like?

Could you feel how much stronger and bigger the energy was at the United Church in the Valley? In this scenario, several things strengthened or deepened the energy, or opened people to it: standing instead of sitting; speaking the gospel from memory so the reader's full attention was on the people, not the book; and the congregation's familiarity with the musical response. The United Church in the Valley also eliminated the pause and full musical introduction between the gospel and the "Hallelujah." Moving immediately and energetically from the gospel to the "Hallelujah" allowed the song to feel like a heartfelt, spontaneous response to the magnificent good news just spoken. At the United Church on the Hill, on the other hand, the words were just as life-giving, but by the time the people began singing (after waiting through the pause and full introduction), they were just singing another song; too much time had elapsed, too much energy had dropped, for it to feel like an authentic response.

Here's another example: The worship leader is reading a story in place of a sermon, a story about hatred and love, about racism and friendship. It is long enough to be read in two parts, at different points in the worship service. The reader ends the first reading at a significant and moving place in the story: An important character has just died. At that moment, the congregation is united in the pain of that death; it brings to the surface the memories of deaths and losses in their own lives. It is very still and quiet in the sanctuary. The leader intends the congregation to slowly and softly begin singing "Were You

There?" and to do so without breaking the energy that moved people to their hearts and bonded the community together. If the mood is not disturbed, the community will naturally sing this haunting spiritual as a lament, an honest response to the pain they are experiencing together at that point in the story. What would that feel like? How would you describe the energy in the sanctuary and in the people at that moment?

Suppose this had happened instead: The reader stops at the same significant place, the congregation is united in the pain, the sanctuary is very still. The silence is broken by the pianist playing a verse of "Were You There?" using the same tempo and volume he might use with any hymn. The worship leader invites the congregation to turn to page 229 and stand to sing. Can you feel how the long introduction, the vigor of the piano music, the spoken invitation, and the insistence on movement (standing up) changes the energy in the sanctuary? It allows everyone to leave the shared pain—in fact, the sudden jerking out of that shared pain is probably abrasive to many folks—and return to their separate thinking minds. Now when they sing, they are no longer voicing an honest and heartfelt lament; they are just singing another hymn.

Imagine a congregation singing "O God, My God"[2] during Lent. The song ends on an unresolved note, allowing the singers to feel the anguish and doubt of the lament and to remember times when they knew such doubt themselves. What does it feel like to end a hymn on an unresolved note? What would be the point of that? Now imagine the organist, who likes cheery music and assumes there is a misprint in the hymnal, resolves the last note. How does that change the energy? How does that feel?

It is possible to chart an entire worship service according to what happens to the *prana* at each point in the service: Some things build it, some things reduce it, some things open our hearts, some things allow us to stay safely in our heads (we'll talk more about heads and hearts later). Of course, not every person will respond in the same way. But certain worship experiences do keep most of us in our heads, in our rational thinking minds. That is not where transformation happens. It is a good place to be during some moments in a worship service, but not all of it, not week after week. Other things in worship do invite or allow or encourage (never force) most of us to move into our hearts or even deeper into our souls; we have all experienced such movement after a stirring choir anthem or a gospel reading that spoke exactly to our own struggles that day.

Leading in Cooperation with Energy in Worship

We have tried to understand a bit about energy in worship, and we looked at several examples and their differing effects on the energy. Now let's talk about the role of the worship leader. Here I look at worship leadership through the lens of energy and its language. This is certainly not the only way to address this or any subject, but it allows us to notice some things that, if we didn't use this particular lens, we would probably not notice. Many worship leaders have an intuitive understanding of these issues, though they may never articulate it or need to. Other pastors will benefit from looking under a microscope at parts of worship leadership that we don't usually think about.

Can you remember a time in your church when the congregation was really together, when you really felt like a community, when the energies of the people gathered were united? Maybe you felt that on Easter morning or after the wonderful celebration of your church's one hundredth anniversary. Maybe you felt that after the tornado came through your town and you gathered to support one another, and to serve. What did it feel like, those moments when the congregation was really united as a community?

Can you also remember a time when that didn't happen? When the energy of the congregation felt scattered and disconnected and never came together, not even by the end of worship? What did that feel like?

I have come to believe that when I am leading worship, it is my job to bring the different, scattered energies together and to re-form the community each week. I want to form a group energy field, as contemporary scientific language might put it; or as our traditional faith language would say, I want to re-form (to re-member) the Body of Christ. It is very important for that to happen in worship so that we can feel our way into trusting that we are one, that we are the Body of Christ. I want it to happen in the first few moments of the service.

Unless I am intentional about this, it may not happen. I have been in many church services (including ones I planned and led!) in which the scattered energies never gelled together. Worship may have been meaningful to individuals, but the people did not experience belonging to a group. In contemporary language, we might say that a group energy field never formed, and so the power and healing of community was not available.

Why does the energy sometimes come together to form a powerful community, and why does that fail to happen at other times? The worship leader serves as a magnet for the disparate energies. I've noticed that when I am scattered and frenzied, it is harder to form that group energy field, but it usually happens easily when I offer a calm and grounded presence.

People come to church with some expectation, often unconscious. At our best, we come expecting—hoping—to feel some love or acceptance from God and the community, to find courage, to discover some meaning in our struggles, to learn how to serve. At the very least, we come as consumers, expecting to be entertained or comforted. When we sit passively through organ music, announcements, and long opening readings, we become restless and nothing draws us out of our separate selves. On the other hand, when something immediately happens that grasps our attention, centers us, or opens our hearts, when we experience something powerful together, the group energy gels, and we become community. For example, a well-chosen poetic call to worship can immediately open our hearts (we'll see some examples later), while artificial, wordy litanies lose our interest, so that we retreat into our busy minds again, our separate spaces. A much-loved opening hymn can change individuals into a community, while a draggy, unfamiliar hymn will not (it's important to learn new music, but the opening hymn is rarely the place to do that).

Often some in the congregation are still shuffling papers, whispering to their neighbors, taking off their coats when the service begins. The energy may remain scattered if the worship leader begins the call to worship anyway, because some of the people are not at all ready to engage yet, and their neighbors are probably distracted by their settling. But these scattered energies are pulled together when the worship leader waits quietly until she has their full attention before reading ... an appropriate response to inappropriate restlessness. Another helpful way to begin worship and to bring the scattered energies together is to name the restlessness and invite people to bring their attention into the present moment, to bring their minds back to the same place as their bodies. This can actually be a very effective call to worship: a gentle invitation to notice our own distractions, to take some slow deep breaths, to pause and center in preparation for worship. When I do this with congregations, I feel a big communal sigh of recognition ("Yes, I am so scattered this morning") and appreciation ("Thank you; I needed to catch up with myself"), and the individuals suddenly become a community.

The way a service begins, therefore, has a large impact on whether or not the community *re*-forms, *re*-members, itself each week. We'll see examples of that as we look at liturgies in later chapters.

One job of the worship leader is to pull people together, to unify all those scattered energies that came into the sanctuary. Another job, one of the most important ones, is to gather all the diverse energies that we are and bring, and give them to God for healing.

As a worship leader, I offer myself as a conduit. I do not create the energy or heal it or control it. But it is my job to know how to gather it, offer it to God, and then return it, healed and strong, to the people.

How does the worship leader gather those energies and give them to God? It happens when that is our intent, named perhaps in our prayer before worship. It happens when the worship leader first stands before the people at the beginning of the service, serving as a magnet for the energies in the room. It happens best when the worship leader is centered and grounded. It happens when the pastor greets the people and begins the service in such a way as to help people trust, open, and relax. It happens on an energetic level, and a skilled worship leader does this. I think this gathering of all the disparate energies is the function that the call to worship is meant to serve.

And how does the worship leader return the healed energies to the people after God does God's thing? This most likely happens at the benediction. It does not seem to happen so well if the benediction is read, with no eye contact, or if the benediction is really a charge instead of a blessing. The benediction is a vital part of the service and has much more significance than just to bring closure to the worship. A benediction is the transfer of blessing, and it is vital to the well-being of the people. The blessing is given by God; the pastor is simply an empty tube, a conduit, carrying God's love, acceptance, and power to the people who so badly need to receive it.

The role of worship leader is, I think, more important than many of us have acknowledged. We see that the worship leader is responsible for pulling the scattered energies together in such a way that an audience becomes a congregation, individuals become a community, and people become the Body of Christ. This is not, of course, all it takes or all it means to be a community, to be the Body of Christ in the world. But here it begins. Here people begin to get a taste of it; here they begin to feel their way into it. These healing shifts happen not because the pastor is a spiritual technician, following some set of rules concerning energy, but because he is a grounded spiritual presence, allowing himself to be used, letting worship do what it naturally does if it is good worship, seeing that nothing gets in the way of the healing, the transforming, that Spirit is aching to do.

Questioning Energy in Worship

I have found that energy language is often meaningful to contemporary folks. It may be new, but it works for them. Still, it raises questions, and I'd like to address a few of those.

Isn't this energy work manipulative? This is a fair question. We could, in a way, charge all worship with being manipulative. Our intent in worship is to change people. We write our sermons with the intention that they will move people from one way of living to another. We sing hymns with the hope that they will open hearts. In ministry, in worship, in the Christian community, we have an agenda. One of the reasons worship leaders have so much power is because we work with tools that are capable of bringing fire, and there is always the possibility that such power can be misused, as we have all seen.

When we pray an *invocation*—invoking, or calling forth, the presence of God—we are doing energy work; we are trying to have an influence. When we pray for war to end and oppression to stop, or when we pray for God to heal a sick child in our midst or bless a young couple beginning their life together, we are doing energy work: We are joining with God to influence the world. One could name any of this manipulative, yet we believe that prayer and healing is the work to which we're called.

The danger always exists that in being aware of the emotions elicited in worship, we manipulate those emotions for our own purposes. That's not the same thing as recognizing emotions and honoring them. If a soloist has just finished a deeply moving song and I let several seconds pass before I slowly, quietly begin to shift the mood in the sanctuary, I am not manipulating; I am honoring. If I ask the organist to play the "Hallelujah" immediately after the Easter gospel without pause or musical introduction, I am creating a service that tries to be authentic, making our actions match the words. I believe that in worship, God is trying to heal people, to open hearts, and to invite the community into justice-making. Energy work is one way to cooperate with God in that effort. For me, it is just a way to be alert: alert to God's movement and alert to my congregation.

All of our spiritual traditions teach us, each in their own ways, to work with energy, though they may not call it that. Centering prayer, the laying on of hands, anointing, deep breathing, communion, baptism, visualization, ritual, the study of chakras, yoga, martial arts, the Buddhist practice of tonglen meditation, the Sufi dhikers, the Hindu mantras, the Catholic Rosary, or the Orthodox Jesus prayer—all these practices (and countless others) involve observing, moving, healing, cooperating with, receiving, or increasing energy. We are involved in energy work whether we name it or not. The best way to keep it from becoming manipulative is to be aware of the movement of energy and the energetic effects of our words, rituals, and actions.

You might say, "I can't be worrying about this all through worship!" Of course not! And you don't have to. Many worship leaders are already working very effectively with energy. They have learned how to design and lead good worship; they understand the movement of energy intuitively, without ever using this language; they are so in touch with themselves (their own fears and hopes, their own ego issues, their own shadow sides), that they do not interfere with energy by using worship to meet their own ego needs. In such worship, Spirit is free to act.

For others, these thoughts may invite them to observe worship more closely, and in doing so, they may notice things they never noticed before: that sudden movement after a moving solo is actually abrasive; that so many words do indeed keep people in a thinking mode; that the benediction transfers healing energy to people, or fails to. Once a worship leader begins to notice these things, needed changes become obvious and often are quite simple.

If you pay attention to energy as you design and lead worship, you may find that it takes up more of your time at first. But that is no different than learning any new skill. Soon you integrate these ideas, and you begin to do them naturally without their requiring you to focus consciously on them during worship.

It has been my experience that when worship leaders design worship in ways that allow the congregation to go more deeply into Spirit, the worship leader herself moves more deeply into Spirit as well. That can begin to happen as she designs worship and continues into the actual service. Of course, the worship leader must stay alert in a way the congregation does not need to, but deeper worship will also, at least at moments, allow the worship leader to go deeper, and in that place there is always renewal. In time, you will lead worship with less worry about it, not more.

Are you equating emotion with energy and maybe with Spirit? That makes me uncomfortable. Me too. First of all, let me say that Spirit is Mystery, something we only catch glimpses of. We cannot define it, possess it, or control it. All language about God is metaphor. Frankly, even energy is a mystery, something we feel but can't really grasp or define. We also know that the relationship between emotion, body chemistry, and attitudes or patterns of thought is complex and not fully understood. I do not equate emotion with Spirit.

My study of energy leads me to believe that emotions may give us helpful information. Depression indicates depleted *prana.* Joy and strength indicate healthy, abundant *prana.* Laughter increases *prana.* Emotions serve as feedback about the state of our energy as individuals or a community. But I do not name the emotion itself as being the same thing as the Holy Spirit, and *prana* or *chi* is something much bigger than our passing emotional states.

How can I learn this? I don't seem to see the movement of energy in worship, or I only see it after someone else points it out to me and labels it. When I try to design worship to work with the chi that is present, I am lost. In this chapter, I try to express in words something for which we have few adequate words. Many of the following chapters offer more concrete tools for creating deep worship. All of it is about working with the energy, whether or not I am using that image. If you learn the things in the rest of this book, you will learn how to work with energy in worship.

Like any new skill, this one takes practice. If you decide to make any changes in your worship, you'll make them slowly, one at a time; and that will give you the space to integrate these new understandings and ideas. You may find books that help deepen your worship and strengthen the *prana*, even though the author may not use that language. If a pastor in your area does worship well, you might invite him to share ideas and resources with you and your clergy colleagues. You will learn a lot by simply observing what happens in your own worship, even before you decide whether you want to make any changes. And of course, look at your own prayer life and the course of your days. Do you get out of your head at some points? Do you learn anything intuitively, or do you only trust intellectual learning? Do you have any space in your day, any silence, any moments of freedom from producing or accomplishing? Living and praying more contemplatively will cause you to see worship in some new ways. It is a process, and Spirit will help you.

If my own pranic energy is very low, how can I help my congregation to have a stronger energy? First of all, work on yourself more than on your congregation. Remember that if you are a pastor, your primary role (whether or not your congregation recognizes this) is to be a spiritual leader for your people, a spiritual presence in their midst, a kind of witness. Being clear about that will help you set priorities more wisely.

What can you do to heal or strengthen or increase your own *prana*? Reread Practice #1 and try one thing at a time, slowly, so as not to overwhelm your already overwhelmed schedule. Could you give something up to slow down your life a bit? One of the pervasive temptations of our culture is to say yes to too many of the very worthy opportunities that we all have today. Maybe you want to consider working with a practitioner of healing energy, one who practices pranic healing or acupuncture or biofeedback or massage. Of course, you already know about looking at your eating habits, sleep patterns, and exercise efforts. Is this the time to begin talking to your congregation about adopting a sabbatical policy?

Meanwhile, trust that God can work through you in spite of your limitations. Your energy does impact your congregation; at the same time, don't be arrogant enough to think good worship is all up to you. Remember, whatever you do helps, but the transforming agent is not your work, but grace. You do a fine thing by being willing to consider these ideas, to think about worship in deeper or broader ways. Not all worship leaders are willing even to do that much. Stay open, do what you can, and trust. God will take what you have to offer, couple it with your sincere intent to have deep worship, and multiply your efforts so as to feed the people.

Isn't there some story about loaves and fishes that fits here?

Practice #3

Move People out of Their Heads

Pastors think people come to church to hear sermons.
They don't. They come to pray and to learn to pray.
—*Eugene H. Peterson*[1]

Contemporary philosopher Ken Wilber says religion serves two functions. He calls one *translation:* helping people cope, make sense of their life, and find meaning in their struggles. The other is *transformation:* helping people to become a Christ, to have the Buddha nature.[2] Most of our worship services offer translation, but not as many do the work of transformation. We need translation; it's absolutely essential. But we need transformation far more: We need to be transformed into disciples of Christ, new beings.

Transformation

Transformation shatters our worldview. It integrates a new consciousness. When one experiences transformation, one perceives reality differently and thus thinks and acts differently. Transformed people live beyond their egos—or are moving in that direction—and recognize that our egocentric sense of separate selves is an illusion. They come to know the profound interconnectedness of life. A direct experience of the Divine becomes possible, as does the capacity to love like Jesus loved. Such transformation is what deep faith and deep worship are about.

Transformation might happen suddenly, but for most of us, it happens gradually (if it happens at all); it is the work of a lifetime. Many things can open us to an experience of transformation: suffering can do it, as can deep prayer, or we might find such an opening in beauty, surrender, present moment awareness, or creation.

We live in an analytical, left-brain society. We are most comfortable in our heads; our thinking, analyzing, comparing, judging selves. Anthropologist Michael Harner describes our culture as *cognicentric*.[3] We certainly do not want to exclude our intellect from worship. Thinking is a vital faith skill. But we are not transformed through our heads. Transformation happens when we move to our hearts or even deeper to our souls; when we come from our hearts and souls, we are open to God and to our neighbors. When our hearts are opened, we are willing to move from our comfort zones. When our souls are touched, we are willing to go deeper into ourselves, willing to uncover what is hidden in us. When we perceive with our hearts instead of our heads, we recognize something bigger than our separate egos. When our analytical minds go off duty for a while, we encounter God.

Some spiritual writers use the word *consciousness* to distinguish between the different mental states we experience. We are in ordinary consciousness when we balance the checkbook, take the kids to soccer practice, or drive to a hospital visit. Teachers of meditation tell us that when we practice deep silence, we move into another kind of consciousness; in this space, we experience life differently. We seem to access a greater creativity. New insights come to us. We know a steady, centering peace, and this deeper consciousness opens us to God more fully than our ordinary mental state is able to do. Transformation happens when we live out of this deeper consciousness. One of the tasks of our faith is to teach us to do that. Such consciousness is particularly familiar to contemplatives, mystics, shamans, and saints, but it's also available to all of us. It is part of our birthright.

The Role of Worship in Transformation

In worship, we want to open people to this deeper reality. We want to invite them into a more profound level of consciousness. We want to make it possible for them to be in their hearts and souls as much as they can. It isn't about forcing people to move into their hearts; it is about making space that invites that movement, space that makes it safe for worshipers to move beyond their defenses and to be vulnerable. Worship should make it possible for people to move from clenched fists to open hands.

So what pieces of worship can shift people out of their heads? Many familiar things do that: silence, deep prayer, music, beauty, chanting. Good poetry, read well, can do it. Worship that is God-centered rather than human-centered can do it. Connecting with the deepest wisdom and practices of other world faith traditions will encourage us to go deeper than our thinking selves. Hearing the stories and wisdom of the ancient saints and mystics can sometimes do it. And the worship leader's own life and prayer may have the capacity to move people from their thinking, egocentric selves to deeper, openhearted stances.

In planning and leading worship, therefore, we need to be mindful of what keeps people in their heads, or jerks them back there, and what offers the space for them to be, if they choose to be, in their hearts, open to a deeper consciousness.

Head-Centered Worship

We begin looking at this issue by recognizing the things in our worship services that allow people to remain head-centered. I will name some things I have noticed and invite you to observe the effect of these in your worship service and in yourself. Remember, when I talk about being in our heads, I am talking about being in our analytical selves, the part of us that judges, compares, critiques, and controls. I encourage you to read this list slowly. As you read, picture worship services you've experienced, and see if what I say rings true for you. The following lists are brief because my purpose here is just to discern how worship keeps us in our heads or takes us into a deeper space. Many of these ideas are illustrated more fully throughout this book.

In a worship service, the following keep people in their analyzing, critiquing selves:

- **Too many words:** When the worship bulletin is full of black type and almost no white space, when the printed call to worship takes up most of the first page, with a long litany at the confession and perhaps another after the offering, we can be sure people are staying in their heads.

- **Many explanations and instructions:** People stay in their heads when we speak to their heads. "Now if you'll turn to page 20, ... Will you stand and sing ... ? I chose this solo because ... ." Some explanations or instructions are occasionally necessary, but frequent ones keep people in their thinking minds.

- **Long, dull readings and poor readers:** Boredom or irritation keeps us in our thoughts, even if the reading might otherwise move our hearts.

- **Distractions:** Noise, shuffling, papers rattling, people roaming in and out, worship leaders who don't seem confident: All these distractions pull people back into their rational minds.

- **Feeling ill at ease or left out:** Visitors who are not welcomed, newcomers who can't follow the service or find the hymns, folks who are overlooked during the passing of the peace: People who are uncomfortable stay in their heads.

- **Moving too quickly or too loudly from a powerful solo (or drama, dance, or reading):** If someone sings a solo that moves us deeply, it takes a moment to return from the deep place to which the music took us. In the powerful silence that follows such a solo, we are no longer in our heads; we have opened our hearts or rested in our souls. If the worship leader too quickly intrudes on that silence or too abruptly shifts the mood, we are abrasively jerked back to ordinary consciousness, as if it were taboo to enter a deeper space during worship.

- **Excess emotion:** The congregant venting his fears about a health problem during sharing time, the pastor speaking with inappropriate intensity during the sermon, or the soloist singing with intemperate feeling: Whenever emotion feels out of control or excessive in worship, we are uncomfortable and we return immediately to our heads, where our defenses are. This does not mean that emotion is out of place in worship; not at all. But frightening or embarrassing emotion will keep people in their heads.

- **Music that is too loud or too soft or too fast or too slow:** A beloved hymn, carrying a lifetime of associations and memories, can quickly move us into our hearts, but if it is played so slow as to drag or so fast that we can't keep up, the inappropriate tempo jerks us back to our heads, the part of us that critiques and feels irritation. If the solo is so loud as to be uncomfortable or so soft that we strain to hear, the discomfort takes us right to our heads.

- **A worship leader who is not centered, who moves too fast, who seems distracted:** God is not limited by our limitations, but if the pastor is not an open channel for the Holy to move through, the people will have a harder time accessing the Spirit.

- **Applause:** Some churches invite applause after an offering of music. One of several reasons I do not like applause in worship is that the noise and movement of applause moves us back into our thought processes.

- **Long silences for which people aren't prepared**: Silence can take us deeper than our heads, but only if people are comfortable with it and if the length is appropriate for the experience of the group.

- **Dimmed lights that come on very suddenly:** At the end of a Good Friday service or after the candlelight singing of "Silent Night" on Christmas Eve, the sudden brightness jerks us abrasively out of the deep places to which the darkness took us.

- **Long music introductions after something moving:** When our hearts have been opened by the powerful, dramatic reading about God's grace, we want to move spontaneously into a doxology, a song of praise. If we must wait through a long musical introduction, the moment passes and we return to our thinking selves.

Perhaps you have never thought of worship like this. But now that you are seeing it this way, you might be able to name other things that keep worshipers in their heads. Let me remind you again that being in our heads for part of the worship hour is as it should be. When we are in thinking mode the whole hour, we come to believe that knowing about God is the same as knowing God. That's a far cry from the life of union with God that Jesus modeled for us.

Heart-Centered Worship

I've named some things that keep people in their thought process-es in worship. What invites people to move into their hearts or rest a few moments in their souls? Well, the opposite of the above examples is obviously likely to do that. The following will give worshipers the space to be in their hearts:

- **Certain music:** We all know how quickly music can open our hearts. It has the capacity to bypass our analytical minds and stir our deepest feelings.

- **Story, drama, dance:** If these are well presented and authentic to worship, they can move us beyond our defenses. This is why Jesus taught through story so much. We get caught up in the story and forget to be on guard, so we hear the truths we normally don't allow ourselves to hear. Also, unlike heady discourses or abstract thinking, story, drama, and dance can reach us regardless of our intellectual skills or educational degrees.

- **Chanting:** This musical form of prayer, different than hymn singing, is valued in all world spiritual traditions because it can quickly move us into the depth of Spirit. Like a mantra in the Buddhist and Hindu traditions, frequent repetitions of a simple sung phrase slow our brain waves and quiet our minds.

- **Silence:** If people are prepared for it, silence can soften people's hearts. It offers a spaciousness that seems to allow us to set down our burdens, pretenses, and obligations and just rest in what is. It offers us the space to be in touch with ourselves again.

- **A sense of calm and safety in the worship space:** Even the atmosphere in the sanctuary can encourage people to put down their defenses and open their hearts (or not). This will happen more often if the space is warm, inviting, beautiful, simple, and uncluttered. Wood, stone, live plants, and natural light enhance the sense of peace.

- **Sitting close, but not too close, to the "power":** Altar, table, font, pulpit: These carry some power, even if it is not consciously perceived. Some people are threatened by this, but others discover that removing the great distance between the focal point of the worship space and the worshiper engages people more fully and makes it more likely that they will be drawn into a heart space.

■ **Speaking instead of reading prayers, benediction, pardon:** When parts of the liturgy are spoken instead of read, they become personal. The worship leader can make eye contact and speak from her heart as if to say, "I really believe I have something to give you, though it isn't my gift, but God's. I want you to have it; I am personally involved in this giving."

■ **Quality poetry, well-chosen and well-read:** Some of the litanies that we often find in worship do not sound like we speak. They are artificially formal and usually quite wordy. Good poetry, on the other hand, cuts right to the chase. However, you must choose it carefully and read it well, both tasks that take some skill. Many people think they do not like poetry, but I have used poetry as part of the liturgy in many churches, and people are hardly aware that I am sharing poetry; they just know that the words grasp their attention and speak to their hearts.

■ **Authentic liturgy:** What is authentic for one tradition may be artificial for another, so this takes some discernment. The following two prayers of confession are both acceptable, but as you read them, notice which one is more likely to move you from your thinking head into an open heart:

> Forgiving God, we come to you humbly and
> contritely, knowing that we have sinned. We know
> that if we confess our sins, we can be forgiven. And
> so we make this confession to you. Sometimes we
> are self-righteous and unforgiving. Sometimes we
> desire revenge or dominance. Forgive us. And
> forgive us when we act out of self-interest. Forgive
> us when we hurt one another, when we fail to care.

> Purge us of the fear that makes us hard-hearted.
> Cleanse us of the arrogance that makes us judge
> others. Free us from the anxiety that makes us
> impatient. And then fill us with your spirit of love
> and compassion. We ask this in the name of Jesus
> who is our Lord and Savior. Amen.

Reading this confession, my mind wandered after only a few lines. There was too much to absorb, and it used ideas that I don't use in daily conversation. I did not really mean what I was saying. Maybe I was supposed to, but I didn't. This prayer was not speaking for me, and I never left my head. Was that your experience?

Now, here is a second confession:

> Sometimes, O God, it is hard for us to wait.
> Sometimes it is even harder to hope.
> Sometimes it is hard for us to believe in new life.
> Forgive us, Lord.
>
> Into our impatience,
> into our hopelessness,
> into our despair,
> we pray that you come. Amen.

Did this move you, even a little bit, out of your thinking self? Did it feel more authentic to you? What differences did you feel as you prayed this prayer and the previous one? Can you name what aspects of each prayer caused you to react differently?

Moving from Head to Heart

Here are some other examples of the difference between worship that confines us in our thinking selves and worship that invites us to move deeper. I begin with a situation we can all recognize; it will help you identify what I mean when I speak of *head* and *heart*.

Imagine that one spring Sunday, worship is built around the celebration of creation. At one point in the service, you use slides or PowerPoint to show beautiful images of creation; your organist plays a musical background to the visuals. The music and the images are moving, and you can sense that the people have shifted into their hearts, into a space of quiet and awe. Suddenly a technical problem develops, and the pictures blink and stutter on the screen. People are jerked from their place of reverence and mystery, jerked back from the experience of *being* to the experience of *doing*.

A new hymn will keep people in their heads as they try to sing it without making mistakes. If the worship planner includes more than one unfamiliar hymn in the service, most people will be in their learning (head) mode most of the hour.

Sometimes the way the bulletin is worded can open us. One line might read, "Scripture: Psalm 40," which is what we expect of the worship aid. But the same line in the bulletin might read like this instead, "God, I'm coming to the party you're throwing for me!" This verse from a paraphrase of psalm 40,[4] used here as a title, surprises us and tweaks our interest. When we come to that place in the order of worship, we're alert and engaged and wondering—all qualities that open us.

If there is a special time for children in the worship hour and it is done well enough so the children participate with attention and eagerness, the people may find themselves quite naturally shifting into their hearts. If the children's time is poorly done, the congregation (not to mention the children) will be impatient or bored—and in their heads.

Once my congregation was wrestling with accepting someone who was different from the rest of us. We were in our heads: feeling discomfort, living in our prejudices, trying to evaluate, voicing our opinions. I invited this person to share a sermon with me one Sunday,

to tell his experience and name some of his struggles. His story, opening our hearts, led to changes in our attitudes and judgments.

The Bible is both history and metaphor. When the history is
emphasized, we stay in our heads. When biblical stories are presented
as metaphor for our own life journeys, we move to our hearts. Both are
important, but the metaphor, more than the history, will move us to
transformation.

If you want to pursue these ideas, I suggest that you begin by simply paying attention to yourself and the congregation during worship.
Can you feel when most of the people tend to be in their heads? Can
you tell when most people seem to be in a deeper place, and do you
know what moved them there? Did you ever notice a moment when
the next item of worship jerked them too suddenly out of their heart
place? When worship is designed in such a way that people move gently back and forth between their heads and hearts, does that feel different than when worship keeps most people in their heads for most
of the hour?

Once you can see this in your own worshiping community, read
the lists in this chapter, and decide on just one thing with which to
experiment for a few weeks. Don't try to rearrange your whole worship
tradition! Start with items that stand out for you or that don't involve
change on the part of someone else, such as your organist. Start with
efforts subtle enough that your congregation won't notice that anything specific was different, but they will make comments about how
meaningful worship was. After you have some good experiences with
a few changes, invite your worship committee or musicians into discussion with you. Help them to discern the difference between head
and heart worship and to recognize the value of worship that invites
people deeper than their thinking selves. Garner their support as you
make more changes.

Notice that these changes do not depend on what kind of worship
your community practices. They are not about becoming more contemporary or staying traditional. They are not about bringing in rock

bands or keeping them out. They are not about whether or not to use PowerPoint in worship; they are not about which hymns to sing. You can continue whatever form of worship your congregation values and deepen it to touch people's souls more fully and open them to God's movement.

I believe that many worship wars happen because so much of our worship has become anemic. It is too head-centered. It is too human-centered. My experience has been that worship that takes people deeper satisfies both the traditionalists and the modernists.

Let me offer a word of caution: Too much heart can be scary. The point is not to turn worship into an emotional extravaganza. We don't need emotion for its own sake in worship; we need the opportunity to go more deeply into our souls. Emotion is sometimes, but definitely not always, a sign of that happening. Without being rigid, I tend to design worship as follows: After a deep, heart-opening experience or something that triggers strong emotion, we move slowly and gently out of that space into something that brings us back to our heads and this reality again. The service becomes an easy flow between head and heart moments, between being in this reality (which feels safe and comfortable) and a deeper one (where healing happens).

Worship is the fireplace that contains the fire that is God. I want to design worship that brings us close to that light and heat, that source of power. I want to make sure that in our worship, we are not so far from the fire that we only know of its glowing because other people tell us about it.

Worship draws on our intellects; and it should. But worship should not be an intellectual event. It is an invitation to transformation, and transformation happens when our hearts open and our souls awaken. I plan and lead worship with that hope, that intent.

Practice #4

Read Scripture
So Nobody's Bored

How do we present Christ to a consumer-oriented,
sex-crazed, self-preoccupied, success-focused,
technologically sophisticated, light-hearted,
entertainment-centered culture?
—*Douglas C. Webster*[1]

In all Christian traditions, the Word is a central part of worship.
We argue endlessly with one another about how to interpret that
scripture, but perhaps that's just proof of how sacred and significant
we consider our holy text to be. I think the Bible can be read on many
levels (historical, metaphorical, literal, devotional, and so on). Each
level of interpretation offers gifts to us, and each way of reading can
also distort scripture if we think it is the only right way to understand
a text. However it is read, the Christian Bible has been the source of
transformation for people and communities for two thousand years.
Some of that transformative power should surely come through when
we hear the Word in worship.

Too often it does not.

We all know what it is like to listen to someone read aloud poorly,
stumbling over words, losing her place, speaking too softly to be heard.
Most pastors and lay readers do much better than that: They speak
loudly, clearly, and with some expression. And yet, if you watch the

congregation during the reading of scripture, you are likely to notice that many people are bored. They may be restless. They are looking around. Their faces reflect disinterest. Few of them appear to be engaged with the text. It would be hard to tell by looking that they are hearing radical, life-giving, transformative, dangerous words. In most of our churches, we don't really expect to be shaken by scripture. Music might open our hearts, and the sermon might stimulate our thoughts, but the scripture? Well, we've heard it before anyway.

I think it is a sin to read scripture in such a way that people are bored.

If you would like to strengthen and deepen your worship, this is a good place to begin. The suggestions in this chapter will have an immediate positive effect on your worship, and they won't threaten anyone. I suggest some basic pointers for effective public reading, and even if you adopt only these recommendations, your scripture will come to life. Then I offer some creative ideas to deepen your congregation's engagement with scripture. All of the ideas presented require some practice, but none require great skill or particular gifts. I wrote this chapter in such a way that it is not only easy to use, but also lends itself for use in training lay readers. And, pastors, don't assume that only lay leaders need this training!

The following are some ways to make the reading of scripture worthy of the words of scripture (these suggestions apply to other readings, as well):

Reading Scripture Well: The Basics

Don't Begin Until You Have the Congregation's Attention

If the people are restless or distracted when you are ready to begin, stand quietly watching the congregation and waiting until they are silent and attentive. (You may recognize this old school teacher trick!) You might feel awkward, at first, but do it anyway: just stand there, saying nothing, until everyone is watching you expectantly.

Don't be embarrassed: scripture deserves their full attention.

If you need some convincing that this is a good thing to do in worship, notice what it is like in the sanctuary when you begin reading the scripture before you have the congregation's attention. What does the energy feel like? How long do you estimate that it took most worshipers to tune into the reading and to catch on to its meaning? How much of it did they miss? On the other hand, notice what the energy is like when everyone is quiet and expectant before the reading begins. Do you believe that scripture is valuable enough to be worth the people's full attention? Don't begin until you have it.

Make Real Eye Contact

When I read scripture to my congregation, I give a priceless gift to people I love. How could I do that without making authentic eye contact with them? Yet most readers hardly look at the congregation when they offer these life-giving words. Perhaps many of us don't really consider scripture much of a gift.

Some readers make no eye contact with the worshipers at all. Many, however, make some effort at it. Most leaders, even clergy, look primarily at the Bible, offering the congregation a quick darting glance now and then by lifting their eyes in the general direction of the people but not really connecting with anyone.

Eye contact means really looking at and into the eyes of specific individuals. That has a very different effect than an occasional generic glance toward the back wall. Real eye contact requires that you know what you are going to read so well, you don't have to be buried in the text. A good reader finds a trick that enables him to look up often without losing his place. You can do this if, for instance, you hold the open Bible on one hand, and use the first finger of your other hand to follow the text as you read. Then, when you look at the people and back to the text, your finger is always pointing at your place.

Without a doubt, it takes some experience and even a little courage to truly look at specific people, because real eye contact is intimate. If you really look deeply at members of the congregation, it will feel intimate even though you will look at each person only a second before you connect with someone else. Many readers are self-conscious enough already without adding another thing to think about, much less something intimate. But with practice, any reader can feel at ease doing this.

When your eyes connect with those of a parishioner, she feels like the scripture is being read just to her; it immediately pulls her into the scripture and brings it to life for her. It also helps her feel that she belongs; in effect, she has been noticed. Eye contact makes people feel that you care for them.

Eye contact can also make someone feel that they are being judged—not by the reader, but by scripture—which means the scripture connected with the congregant's life; that's good. I find that when this happens, most people are ready to receive that judgment; it startles them into an awareness that they are ready to face. I do exercise some caution in this regard, however. If a church member was in my office on Wednesday confessing to adultery, I avoid looking at him as I read about David and Bathsheba on Sunday morning. If I listened to a parishioner's grief on Thursday, I may in fact look at her on Sunday as I read the comforting words of Psalm 23. I don't make a big project out of whom to look at and whom to avoid; it just comes naturally when I am sensitively aware of my people and their pain.

If you have a large sanctuary with a lot of space between the lectern or pulpit and the people, genuine eye contact is much harder. You can't make eye contact with people in the back pews when you can barely see them. But you can do it as best you can. You can look in the eye of those who are closer, and look toward those seated farther away. It is worth the effort: When you read scripture, make real eye contact.

Come Among the People to Read

I suspect it is no accident that in many churches, there is a great distance between the Word (symbolized by the pulpit, altar, robed clergy) and the people sitting in the pews. Regardless of our rational thoughts, there is some intuitive awareness that at the place near the altar, the table, and the Bible, there is a lot of power. People don't want to get too close. When you read scripture, you want to reduce that distance as much as possible; you want to get the Word into the people's lives, not on the periphery. So if you are able to do so, consider walking into the congregation for the reading of scripture. Stand amidst the people to read this life-giving Word.

But there are a couple things for you to consider. If your pulpit is miked but you are not, you are probably tied to the pulpit. If that is the case, I suggest that you begin talking with the appropriate committee about your sound system. Even a simple and inexpensive upgrade can give you more freedom to move from the pulpit and still be heard. Why should a microphone be in charge of worship?

Some of your people have hearing difficulties. They may hear better when you are in the pulpit because your voice is projected toward them and your lips and facial expressions are clearly visible. If you walk down the aisle of your sanctuary, you may end up standing behind some people, and even if you have a mike, a few may not be able to hear you well. Talk to your people and experiment with this so you don't lose more than you gain. Even if you just walk away from the pulpit and stand free or take just a few steps toward the people, it will help to remove the space barrier that allows people to distance themselves from the Word.

As much as possible, come among the people to read.

Read Like You Talk

Talk to a friend for a moment, and then pick up your Bible and read in the same tone of voice you used when talking to your friend. When you read scripture in church, use your normal voice, not your Bible voice. Read like you talk.

For some reason, most people do not do this. When they read the Bible, their voices change; the tone changes, perhaps the pitch. They may not read in a monotone, but the inflection is different than the inflection of their normal conversational voices. Don't take my word for it; start listening. Listen to yourself and others reading scripture in church and talking in the course of the day. Notice the differences. When you talk, do you speak louder or softer, depending on the content of what you're saying? Do you speak sometimes slowly, sometimes quickly, depending on the emotion of the moment? When you speak, is each word evenly paced, or do you sometimes pause after you say something very important? Once you can hear everyday speech, you are ready to try to read like you speak.

It might be easiest to work with this if you find a scripture story that has characters and emotion in it. When you read, do the characters sound arrogant, scared, awed, confused, grief-stricken, excited? They should. Do the character's words sound different than the narrator's words? They should. Look at Luke 22:54–62, for example. This is the powerful story of Peter's denial. How would Peter sound in verses 57, 58, and 60? Scared? Angry, to cover being scared? Gruff? Would he say, "Man, I do not know what you are talking about!" slowly, with each word spaced evenly, or would he speak fast, the words running together? Notice the pitch. Many readers use the same pitch for all sentences (this is part of the Bible reading voice), but isn't it more authentic for Peter's pitch in this sentence to drop at the end?

Notice that in normal speech, we alter the tone and the tempo depending on our emotion; for example, we speak more quickly when we are excited and more slowly when we are trying to understand a new idea. When we read scripture, we can do the same. We might read some lines very slowly, especially if they are important or if they carry difficult ideas, as in some of Paul's letters. We read other lines more quickly than normal, especially those that are easy to understand or that convey joy or excitement. Experiment with Psalm 23. Perhaps you'd read verse 1 slowly, but read verse 3 a little more quickly, emphasizing the joy. Maybe you'd slow a bit in verse 4. Remember that you can use pauses for emphasis, though that takes some practice to do well.

Learning to read well is harder to read about than to do, because all of us already speak naturally in ways that convey emotion. We don't need to learn how to do that. We just need to recognize that for reading to come to life, it must sound authentic and natural like our speech does. You might listen to an audio book. Notice how the voice changes in pitch, tone, and tempo. Notice how the voice matches the words. Can you hear the ways the voice conveys emotion? Can you hear changes in the voice as emotions alter? Of course you can hear the difference between tenderness and rage. Aside from the meaning of the words, what about the voice conveyed those differences? Can you identify times when the reader used pauses for emphasis?

Once again, let me reassure you. Thinking about strange things like the pitch of your voice, listening to audio books: this sounds like a big project. It is not, though, because there is nothing to learn; you already do it perfectly well. I just offer some ways for you to become aware of something you may not have thought about so you can confidently begin to read the way you speak.

Remember, excess emotion always makes people uncomfortable, and that will immediately pull them out of the story. Readers most often err on the side of reading with little or no emotion, but when they are invited to try to put normal emotion into the reading, especially into verses that relate someone's conversation, the temptation is to err on the side of excess. Practice carefully. Practice with a family member or friend, and ask for their feedback. In public worship, emotion in your reading needs to be genuine and natural but also contained. Scripture will come to life if you read like you talk.

These are the basics for reading scripture (or anything else) well: Don't begin until you have the people's attention. Make real eye contact. Come among the people to read. Read like you talk. If you make just these changes in your reading, you will improve worship enormously.

Reading Scripture Well: Beyond the Basics

If you are a little adventuresome, you can do some other things to make sure no one is bored when you read scripture, which makes it possible for people to really engage with these words of life. We all recognize that many art forms can bring scripture to life: music, drama, visual art, puppets, and liturgical dance, for instance. I encourage the use of these things. But here I offer simple techniques that any reader can try, though if you are a lay reader, you will need to check with the pastor, worship planner, or musician before you use any of them in a service.

Intersperse Music with Scripture

For example, on Maundy Thursday, you might read the story of Jesus in Gethsemane as recorded in Mark 14. Begin by reading verses 32–34. Then the congregation can sing the Taizé chant "Stay with Me,"[2] which is based on this scripture. After they repeat this chant a few times, they might continue to sing very softly while you read verses 35–38. The chant can continue while you pause; then perhaps when the chanting stops, you finish with verses 39–42. If you do this, it is important to do any explaining before this part of the service begins so the flow of the service is not interrupted with instructions. After you do this kind of thing a few times, your congregation will not need explanations each time.

If your gospel reading for the day included Jesus' words about being salt and light in Matthew 5:13–16, you could immediately follow that reading with "You Are Salt for the Earth, O People," by Marty Haugen.[3] Consider inviting the people to find the page in the hymnal before you begin reading so the congregation can hear the scripture and then sing the hymn without the break in mood and attention that will happen if people must hunt for hymnals and turn pages. Consider asking your organist not to play the entire hymn as an introduction, because a long time lapse between the hearing and the singing of the scripture will break the connection between the two.

You might alternate verses of a hymn and verses of scripture. Evenly alternating reading and singing for four verses usually doesn't work; we need more variety to hold our attention. Try reading one verse and singing two, reading the remaining scripture, and then singing a final verse. Or read Psalm 100:1–2 and sing the first verse of "All People That on Earth Do Dwell."[4] Another example uses the Magnificat in Luke 1:46–55: Begin by singing the first three verses of "My Soul Gives Glory to My God,"[5] read verses 46–51, sing the third verse of the song, finally read the rest of the Magnificat and sing the last two verses. If you combine hymns and scripture like this, the congregation should remain seated during the singing. Sitting and standing would be much too disruptive.

Of course, an old and wonderful practice is having the pianist play softly in the background during the reading. This often stirs emotions! Consider, for example, the reader beginning with Isaiah 49:14–16, the scripture that tells us that God holds us in the palm of God's hand. After a few phrases, the piano comes in, very softly playing "Wondrous Love."[6] Music used this way is usually played at a slower tempo than if people were singing. In that case, when the reading is done, the pianist can increase the tempo to lead the congregation into singing the hymn. Once again, invite the people to open their books before you begin.

Use Echoing to Engage the Congregation in Scripture

This is another useful tool. As you read the scripture passage, repeat an important word or phrase, and then invite the congregation to repeat it before you continue the reading. Keep the pace fast enough that you don't break the flow. Use simple hand signals to invite the congregation to echo a word or phrase, to continue chant-style instead of saying the word just once, to chant louder or softer, and finally to stop. This is very simple, fun to do, and usually quite powerful. Here is an example. Remember that what seems complicated in print is actually easy to do. The passage is Romans 8:35–39 (omitting verse 36), with those words that the congregation would echo in bold.

> Who will separate us from the love of Christ? Will
> **hardship,** or **distress,** or **persecution,** or **famine,** or
> **nakedness,** or **peril,** or **sword**? **No** (*repeated loudly
> several times*), in all these things we are **more than
> conquerors** through him who **loved us.** For I am
> **convinced** that neither **death, nor life, nor angels,
> nor rulers, nor things present, nor things to
> come, nor powers, nor height, nor depth, nor
> anything else** (*read and echo this section one phrase at
> a time; you can shorten it by combining two words or
> phrases, but that is less powerful*) in all creation, will
> be able to separate us from **the love of God**
> (*repeated softly several times*) in Christ Jesus our
> Lord.

Invite the Congregation to Make Sound Effects

For the reading of Acts 2 or Ezekiel 37, ask your parishioners to participate by making the sound of the wind. Matthew 2 invites a rhythmic clapping that represents the sound of camel hoofs. Parts of the Exodus story could be read while people moan very softly. In the background of the Passion story, the congregation could chant a soft, repeated "Crucify him!" Instruct the congregation to get louder or softer or stop suddenly according to your hand signals. Something as simple as providing sound effects can pull the people into the story.

Print the Scripture as a Script

If you print the scripture as a script, the congregation can participate. You might print it in the bulletin. If it consists of two or three voices, divide the congregation appropriately. Each part of the congregation reads the correct section, which you already marked. For example, you might say, "Choir, read the narrator's part; gospel side, read the rich man's words; and you folks on the epistle side, read Jesus' lines."

If you have some fairly good readers in the congregation, make one script for each part, with the words for that part clearly highlighted. Pass out the marked scripts before church or even during worship. For example, you might say, "We're going to read the prodigal son story, but I need your help. Who wants to read the father's part?" Of course, you can also turn scripture into scripts that you give to readers beforehand so they can practice. This is necessary if the reading is difficult, contains hard-to-pronounce names, or if you don't have people who are able to read well without warning.

When you turn a reading into a script, make it simple and direct. Eliminate excess words such as "he said" or "she said." Type the script in a large font with white space between each different voice so people who do not have an opportunity to practice will find it easy to read.

Use Reader's Theater

Reader's theater is a powerful way to read scripture, though it takes practice and participants will need to rehearse in advance. In reader's theater, you not only have different voices, but they may also overlap, with people speaking different lines at the same time or everyone saying some lines together. Treat the human voice as an instrument, and teach people to vary their voices, sometimes sounding louder, sometimes softer. Reader's theater is most effective if, instead of standing in a straight line, the readers place themselves in different parts of the sanctuary, or stand in a circle with their backs to one another, or stagger the heights of the people, some sitting on stools, some standing. You might invite the readers to wear all black or to wear blue jeans and white shirts. You may find reader's theater pieces in print, but you will often have to write your own. It is worth the effort.

Memorize Scripture to Bring It to Life

It can be very meaningful to the congregation if the worship leader speaks the scripture from memory. People pay attention! This is especially effective if you can come from behind the pulpit, moving a little as you speak or walking into the midst of the people. This takes some work—and a little courage! I find it helpful to type the reading in a clear font with sections divided by white space, like paragraphs. I try to type one phrase or idea per line, like poetry, because the visual structure helps me remember the lines. I put the reading on stiff paper or cardboard and carry it around with me for the week or for the day or two before worship, so I can practice it in any spare moments of the day: waiting at a red light, sitting in the doctor's office. At worship, I usually have my script in my hand in case I need it; my goal is not to show off my perfect skill but to wake people to this gospel.

The living Word has the power (the intent) to transform us, but for that to happen, we may need to hear it in new ways so we can receive the life it brings. I invite you to watch your congregation as scripture is read; see how the people respond; notice whether or not they are engaged. If the Word does not seem to be life-giving for your people, you might try some of the ideas in this chapter to see for yourself if they make a difference.

Practice #5

Make Every Part Match

**(P)eople are not hungry for more worship services,
for more hymns, sermons and anthems.
They are hungry for an experience of God.**
—Thomas G. Long[1]

Some faith bodies—Catholics, Lutherans, Episcopalians, and Orthodox, for instance—follow a set order of worship, beautiful and sacred words that shape worship. Others, such as most Quakers, do not have an elaborate order of worship. Still other traditions in our Christian communion have the option of varying worship from week to week. Most of these churches probably have an order of worship that they have used for many years without too much variation. The template is in the computer, and from week to week, they only need to change the hymn numbers, sermon titles, and scripture reading.

For some worshipers, this sameness can be boring; for others, it is comforting. Sometimes the order of worship itself becomes an idol, and no one dares to change anything; at other times, the desire to be creative eliminates the stability and depth that comes from familiar structures or repeated responses.

Whether your worship structure is prescribed by your tradition or whether you are free to create your own structure is not the issue. In either case, you can plan worship in a way that invites people into a deeper space if you honor this suggestion: To whatever extent you have a say in the content of worship, make all the parts of the worship service match. To help understand what that means and looks like, let's consider a service in which the parts do not match.

Suppose the opening hymn is a good one, a wonderful song praising God. The call to worship draws on the theme of our coming together in spite of our differences. During the children's time, the children learn the story of Daniel and the lion's den, a story about trusting God. The choir sings a fine anthem about prayer. The gospel is Luke's story about the healing of the blind man, and the sermon is about healing. The final hymn is about going forth to serve. We can assume that each part of this service was marvelously well done, faithful, and authentic. But in an hour, at least six different themes have been offered: praise, community, trust, prayer, healing, and service. The service likely felt choppy, and people probably stayed in their heads most of the time to keep up with constantly shifting ideas.

When worship involves many muddled themes, worshipers do not experience a unified worship; they just experience many nice parts. I counted the themes in a service one holiday weekend: patriotism (in a hymn), dedication of a new baptismal font (ritual prayers), welcoming a new staff member (children's time), Jesus as the good shepherd (scripture and hymn), and the experience of Spirit in our lives (sermon). This kind of worship mimics the fast-paced sound bite style of our culture, which is not, as a steady diet, the way to move deeper.

Worship planners often make some effort to build around a theme, and so the scripture, sermon, and middle hymn may support one another; however, the theme is not repeated anywhere else. The soloist chose her music without regard to the day's scripture, and the man leading children's time acted independently in choosing the story he reads.

I find that when all of the parts of the worship service support one another and communicate a single message as much as possible, people are able to move more deeply into the service and into their faith, and they are more likely to remember the gospel message when the worship is over.

The task of the sermon or homily is traditionally to proclaim the gospel; therefore, I find it useful to think of the whole service as the sermon. Those who do not pay much attention to the preaching will still get the gospel message in the hymn or absorb it from the children's time. In my congregations, laypeople have noticed and articulated that the whole service is a sermon. Yes! The music and the readings and the liturgical dance and the children's time—each proclaims the gospel message of the day. I smile when people tell me how much they liked my sermon on a Sunday when there wasn't one! That is, I may not have preached the gospel for ten or fifteen minutes in the traditional manner. But the readings, a skit or story, music, and short comments throughout the service all proclaimed and explained the scripture. There wasn't a traditional "sermon," but it was all sermon.

Worship That Matches: What It Looks Like

Let me demonstrate what such a carefully crafted service might look like. The worship leader studies the lectionary text or chooses the scripture she will use. Every scripture has multiple possibilities, so next she must decide on a theme on which to focus. For instance, if we read the story of Jesus feeding the five thousand in Matthew 14, the theme could be the miracles of Jesus, the goodness of God, the power of sharing, the problem of world hunger, or the exclusion of women, to name just a few possibilities. If the service is to be sharply focused, the worship leader must choose only one of those themes.

If, for instance, the pastor chooses to focus on world hunger, the call to worship and the offering prayer will include references to world hunger. The opening hymn might be a praise hymn, but others should be about caring for our neighbors, serving, being one family, or discipleship in the world—themes that hold us to our focus on world hunger. The children might learn something about world hunger or the gospel story of Jesus feeding the five thousand. Litanies or readings would be about world hunger. The choir anthem might be about Jesus' care for the poor or his call to follow him in service. The sermon or the charge should help us know what we can do about world hunger and inspire us to do it. The entire service becomes one unit, with everything supporting everything else and each piece in the order presenting one specific message of the gospel. This focus helps to reduce the scattered, distracted thinking of the people, and it emphasizes one message that will likely get through to everyone in some part of the service. I think of this as tending to the integrity of the service.

Here's another example: Suppose I am preaching from Matthew 18:21–35, "Lord, ... how often should I forgive?" My theme is obviously forgiveness, and so that is (as much as possible) the focus of every part of the service. There is a prayer of confession and an assurance of pardon. For the children's time, I talk about forgiving our siblings or friends after they hurt us, or I might read a story about forgiveness. I ask the soloist to sing something about forgiveness if possible or perhaps about God's grace and mercy. In prayer or litany, I will again name our struggle to be a forgiving people. I might use reader's theater or offer a powerful reading about forgiveness. The first hymn and call to worship may be words and music of adoration, but the other hymns would be about forgiveness or God's mercy and grace. The bulletin may include a quote about forgiveness. If I want to be very clear about the theme, I may distinguish between our accepting God's forgiveness and our forgiving one another, themes that, though related, each have their own issues.

Suppose we are dedicating a new organ, digital piano, or set of drums in worship. I might build the whole service around music as a form of prayer and praise, and we would sing hymns of praise. I'd talk to the children about how people use many kinds of instruments, including the human voice, to praise God. Perhaps we would read Psalm 150: "Praise the LORD! ... Let everything that breathes praise the LORD!" Maybe we would build the service as a hymn sing, tracing the history of Christian music through hymns, with soloist and choir presenting Gregorian chants, contemporary praise songs, or other music not in the hymnal.

It is my experience that when all parts of the service are so connected, and every part supports the same clear focus, people feel calmer, become more centered, and are more likely to move from their heads into their hearts and souls.

If your church says Mass or follows a prescribed office, this is less of an issue, but it is still important. You can see that the sermon, hymns, solos, and any elective readings carry just one theme. Remember that it is not only the words and music that convey a gospel message. You can use art to communicate the theme too: banners, paintings, or fabric art, visuals on the altar or table, the pictures in the bulletin. In fact, these avenues are vital ways to communicate; and whether you have a little or a lot of freedom in designing your liturgy, I urge you to consider how the worship space can change from week to week to preach the gospel visually. However you do it, make the entire service one unit in which everything supports everything else and presents one specific gospel message.

Sometimes, though, it is not practical or even possible to make every part of worship match. Perhaps there is a baptism scheduled for Epiphany, and so you already have two themes. Or maybe your congregation values some Mother's Day traditions, but you are also tied to the lectionary reading for the day, which is another theme altogether. Don't worry about what you can't change! Sometimes you can minimize the lack of focus by putting different themes in different places in the service, instead of interspersing them, so that for the baptism, there is the ritual, a reading, and a baptismal hymn, but the rest of the service matches the scripture or season. And, of course, you can try to find creative ways to combine themes that at first seem to have little or no connection. I had the delight and privilege of baptizing my grandson, and the day that worked for our family happened to be the first anniversary of 9/11. I did not want to tarnish the celebratory nature of the baptism with the painful memories of the previous year, but I could not ignore the anniversary date, either. So I built a joyful service around baptism, with my sermon focusing on the question and answer: *What do we do in times of crises? We baptize a child,* thus emphasizing our refusal to turn over our future to despair. It does not matter that sometimes the service can't all match the same theme, but it is worth the effort to see that most of it matches most of the time.

Worship that Matches: How to Plan It

Speaking of effort, I want to acknowledge that this way of planning worship may be more difficult, especially if this is new for you. You cannot create an order of worship weeks ahead and just plug in the sermon title; and you have to be clear about the focus early enough that the musicians or dancers or artists can plan their work. It takes some time to search for readings or litanies that fit the focus. However, I find it very rewarding to work this way, not only because of its effect on worshipers, but also because of its impact on me. Designing worship with matching parts allows me to go more deeply into one theme, and I find that I remember the focus long after that Sunday passes. Because I was so immersed in the theme of hospitality, for example, I find that weeks after that service, I still notice poetry, articles, quotes, or insights about hospitality. They seem to jump off the page or screen at me; my awareness has sharpened. I may have originally shaped the service around hospitality to the stranger as a Christian spiritual practice, but now I discover moving resources about hospitality to different parts of ourselves, especially the parts we don't like; and so I plan another service around that image. I find that this method of crafting a service allows both the congregation and the worship planner to explore the themes of our faith more deeply.

To craft a service in which everything matches, the worship leader and the musicians must work together. In some churches, that can be a serious challenge! Musicians have their own visions—and their own problems and obstacles—and they don't want to add one more limitation. Sometimes pastors and musicians make a great team, with each supporting and enhancing the other's contribution to worship. If that is not the case in your church, you will need to move slowly, learn to listen, and try to get a glimpse of your musicians' vision so you can work *with* them instead of *against* them. If you practice your relationship skills, in time you can help the musicians understand your efforts to deepen the meaning of worship. It might be useful to have the worship committee involved in learning how to deepen and revitalize worship, broadening the ownership of these liturgical efforts.

It takes more time to ensure that the parts of the service carry the same theme. I make that challenge easier by choosing tentative themes a few months in advance or for a particular liturgical season. I gather a file folder for each Sunday, write the date and theme on the tab, then when I come across a possible resource, I put it in the folder. While hunting for a call to worship for this Sunday, for instance, I see one that fits wonderfully with the theme I chose for May 17, so I copy or make a note of its source and drop it in the folder for May 17. While reading a novel, I come across a story that might be just what I need to illustrate a point in the service on May 24; I make note of the story and drop it in that folder. When I'm planning for a rich and interrelated time such as the season of Advent, or the special services during Holy Week, or a sermon series, I may use inexpensive plastic baskets that are big enough to hold not only my notes but also a few books or items I want to use for children's time. I label each basket and line them up on a shelf or table, making it easy to collect abundant resources and notes for upcoming worship services. This habit makes it possible for me to find appropriate resources that I might not otherwise have the time to hunt for.

Make every part match. For me, this way of designing worship is rich and rewarding. For my congregations, it allows them to go deeper into worship and to hold the gospel more firmly in their hearts and lives.

Practice #6

Use Fewer Words

Religion is an attempt to gesture with words toward what is beyond words. It is a dialogue with silence through icon, text, and liturgy. If religion refuses its servant role of bringing the worshiper ever more deeply into silence, if it points to itself, it muffles the silence.

—Maggie Ross[1]

Some of us, especially those of us in Protestant churches of the old mainline traditions, like words. Our sermons are long, our prayers are wordy, our bulletins are full of ink. We like words because we like thinking. We are most at home in our heads, and words are the tools we know. How ironic that in church we use so many words to talk about Something that is beyond all words!

The worship bulletins I created in my early years of ministry are full of words: litanies, unison prayers, responsive readings. But bulletins from more recent years have a lot of white space. I love words. I am a preacher, a reader, and a writer. I use words as icons, an art form that takes one through and beyond the form and into God. But when it comes to opening ourselves to God, I have learned that less is more.

Some traditions—Catholic, Episcopal, Lutheran, for instance—build their services on historic words, a prescribed order of worship. This is not my tradition, but I have worshiped and even ministered in these denominations. I am certain the power and beauty and familiarity of ancient words can invite one into deeper places of Spirit if the worship is designed with that intent. In part, the familiarity of the liturgy moves people out of their thinking selves, a bit like praying a mantra. However, in this chapter, I address those churches that create worship anew each week or at least choose readings and prayers to insert into a familiar order of service. When we are designing our own worship and using new liturgy every Sunday, we need to remember to use fewer words if we want to invite people to move more deeply into their hearts and souls.

I have a passion for worship that does just that: opens people to their hearts and souls. A few words used judiciously can indeed take us out of our heads; mantras and chants are clear examples of that. But reading an excess of words usually keeps us head-centered because it requires us to think. Worship is deeper when we use words more sparingly.

Space through Prayer and Liturgy

I am going to give you two examples—both prayers of thanksgiving after communion—that I wrote and used in worship services. Both have merit. Imagine that you are reading these prayers aloud and in unison during worship. This is the first:

> Lord, you who feed and sustain us, we give you
> great thanks for this sacred feast. We thank you
> that you have welcomed us at your table, that you
> have fed us the sacred food, that you have filled us
> with yourself. We thank you that you have called us
> into community to share this table with one
> another. We thank you that you have loved us, and
> love us still, and will love us always. We thank you
> that you have called us to be your people. Amen.

How did you respond to this prayer? Did you absorb all the ideas? Did your mind wander?

Now here's the second prayer:

> Holy One, we have feasted at your table,
> we have filled ourselves with love.
>
> For the gifts of this table,
> for the community gathered,
> for life,
> we give you great thanks. Amen.

Both prayers are sincere, both are poetic, both might be good liturgy. But the first one has three times as many words as the second.

What happens to us as worshipers when we wade through long unison readings? I think our minds often begin to wander, even as we speak the words aloud. The many words and images begin to blur together. We can't take them all in at once, so even though we're saying the words, we are not absorbing much of the meaning. The second prayer example cuts to the chase. Even the way it is printed on the page, with white space around it and each phrase standing alone, helps us to absorb the images or ideas it presents. In fact, the first prayer would work better if it were printed in that same fashion instead of in paragraph form:

> Lord, you who feed and sustain us,
> we give you great thanks for this sacred feast.
> We thank you
> that you have welcomed us at your table,
> that you have fed us the sacred food,
> that you have filled us with yourself.
> We thank you
> that you have called us into community

> to share this table with one another.
> We thank you
> that you have loved us,
> and love us still,
> and will love us always.
> We thank you
> that you have called us to be your people. Amen.

Do you find this easier to follow than the same prayer written in paragraph form? Does the writing style help you more easily focus your attention and absorb the meaning? If you saw these prayers when you opened your worship bulletin, one written in paragraph form, the other in verse with white space around it, would one seem to invite you in more than the other?

Look at another example, this time a call to worship. The first is written in a traditional style:

Leader: Come! It is time to worship.

People: We come from near and far. We come eager, and we come tired. We come rejoicing, and we come despairing. We come hurting, and we come hoping.

Leader: You are welcome here. This is a place to rest and a place to be healed.

People: We come wanting God to speak to us.

Leader: This is a place of love; listen for God's whisper or God's shout.

People: We come wanting to be in community.

Leader: This is a place of community, not perfect, but faithful.

People: We come wanting to serve, to be of use in the world, to be God's instruments.

Leader: This is a gathering of servant people, offering ourselves as the hands of Christ to heal the broken, to free the prisoners, to welcome the lost.

People: Come! Let us worship together.

Even this is shorter than many calls to worship I have experienced (and written). It is not bad liturgy; in fact, it has some lovely phrases and images, but it is long. Does it take you out of your head? As one of the first things to happen in worship, does it pull you into the service with eagerness, or do you just speak it mechanically, waiting politely for the parts of the service that do engage you?

It is important to have some readings that the congregation shares; worship needs to be participatory. But the next example, spoken by the worship leader, offers one alternative to the traditional wordy call to worship. It is a modern rendering of the words of St. Francis.

> God came to my house and asked for charity,
> And I fell on my knees and cried,
> "Beloved, what may I give?"
> "Just love," God said, "just love."[2]
> Come, let's worship the God who calls us to love.

This call to worship uses words more sparingly, but did you notice any other difference between the two examples? Which one grasped your attention? Did one bring you out of your thoughts and into the present moment more than the other?

Space in the Worship Bulletin

Let's focus on the bulletin or worship aid for a moment. Thomas G. Long, in his book *Beyond the Worship Wars*, describes bulletins as "expressions of hospitality, guides to newcomers unfamiliar with the words and actions of worship, maps for travelers venturing into a new and strange land."[3] In this way, bulletins are a service. They allow the congregation to participate in spoken prayers or readings. But bulletins can also get in the way of worship. Worship asks that we live in the present moment with awareness; God, after all, is not found in the past or the future, but only in the Eternal Now, which is the present moment. When we have a bulletin in our hand, we keep leaving that space to look back at the printed order of worship to see what comes next. With a bulletin, we spend time reading instead of worshiping.

In a church I visited one Sunday, the worship bulletin was sixteen pages long, with three additional inserts. There is some justification for this: Visitors and people with hearing difficulties may find it helpful to have the scripture lessons printed: new songs copied in the bulletin (with copyright permission) expand the musical repertoire of the congregation; and announcements are an important part of a community's life. But on this particular morning, I watched people turning pages, flipping insert sheets, hunting for where they were supposed to be; in those moments, they were not present in worship, and they were not free to move into a deeper space of Spirit. This bulletin in our hands was a booklet, encouraging us to worship by reading, which eliminates the possibility of moving to a place beyond words. And, although some of those sixteen pages and three inserts were announcements, the liturgy itself was also very wordy. In a one hour service, the people had six litanies to read aloud together, which took up sixty-five lines of print. That is too many words!

I encourage you to think about your bulletin. Does it enhance worship or prevent it? Does it invite people deeper than their thinking selves or sabotage efforts to move deeper? Does the bulletin model space? Or does it model fullness, busyness, crowdedness, noise? Does your bulletin convey frenzy or serenity? The reason I use a lot of white space in bulletins is because it becomes a visual model of what I hope worship will be: a place offering some structure that allows God and the worshiper to show up in the same place at the same time, but not too much structure because once they are there together, God and the worshiper can handle it on their own.

One Sunday, I was preaching about our efforts to make God into something we can control. I used the line from *The Lion, the Witch and the Wardrobe* that describes the lion Aslan, the Christ figure in this novel, "Safe? ... Who said anything about safe? 'Course he isn't safe. But he's good."[4] I decided to use the bulletin as part of the message, so although the outsides of the bulletins looked normal, the insides were completely blank. I instructed the greeters to distribute the bulletins as usual, making no sign that anything was different. When people got to their seats and opened their bulletins, they assumed they received one that didn't go through the copy machine correctly and went back for another. The greeters were to simply say, "Oh, sorry!" and hand them a new bulletin, which, of course, was also blank. By the time worship began, I had the congregation's attention! The blank bulletins became a playful but very effective tool to remind us that God, like Aslan, is not a tame lion. God is not predictable and under our control. We cannot always know what is happening, but we are called to live in trust. On that Sunday, using no words was a powerful way to communicate.

Watch your community, and notice how the bulletins affect worship. Their use is both a blessing and a curse; but if you observe their impact in your worship setting, you may notice things you never noticed before. Then you can find ways to minimize the drawbacks of bulletins. Perhaps you can distribute them some weeks and not others. Maybe you can shorten them. Can you reduce the wordiness of your liturgy? Maybe you can invite people, at certain points of the service, to put their bulletins down and just be present to worship.

Space in the Worship Service

Faith is not a matter of intellectual concepts (though our Western faith has too often been just that). Faith is experiencing the living God moving in one's life; faith is making a commitment to that God. When Christians or people of other faiths go deeply enough into prayer, go deeply enough into their faith, go deeply enough into an experience of the Reality we name God, they uniformly report that they go beyond words, which means beyond concepts and ideas. Deep prayer ultimately leads most of us to silence, because there are no words for what we experience of God. I sometimes think that we use so many words in church to cover the realization that though we know all about God, we do not know God.

Faith demands space. Using fewer words in liturgy gives space to the worshiper. The bulletin can help you offer space. There are other ways as well. Sometimes, of course, it comes in the form of silent prayer. Sometimes it comes in the several seconds the pastor allows after a moving solo before shifting to the next part of worship. Sometimes there is space after the sermon before we move on. Sometimes the space is present in the way the worship leader moves. For example, at the Good Friday services in churches I've served, we do the readings and music, snuff out one candle for each of the seven last words, and strip the altar. We have relived the crucifixion of Jesus, and we sit in darkness except for the flame of the one Christ candle. I read the few lines from Luke 23 about the burial of Jesus, ending with "This man went to Pilate and asked for the body of Jesus. Then he took it down, wrapped it in a linen cloth, and laid it in a rock-hewn tomb." I just sit for a moment, sit in the midst of all the expectancy, when everyone knows what I am about to do, but holds their breath waiting for me to do it. Then I stand. I pause before I walk slowly to the candle. I pause again, holding the raised snuffer above the light. I pause once more after I take away the light of Christ. These moments—only a second or two—give people space to be present, to feel, to take in. I did this intuitively and would not have thought much about it if worshipers hadn't brought it to my awareness, telling me how meaningful that slow, deliberate sequence was. They were right. Had I just gotten up after the reading and walked normally to the candle, snuffing it out without hesitation, the worshipers would simply have been observers at a church service. As it was, because of the drama of my slow, intentional, wordless movements, they became mourners at the foot of the cross. Something deeper than their heads was engaged. Sometimes movement and absence of movement say more than any words can say. Use fewer words.

I named silent prayer as one way to allow space in worship. Let me return for a moment to the issue of silence. How much silence is there in your worship? Is there any opportunity for people to simply slow down, let go of *doing,* and just rest in God's presence? Corporate worship is not the same thing as a prayer service. There will be less space and silence in community worship than in a gathering for prayer. But there should be some space; there should be some silence. Many of us are afraid of that silence—or at least unused to it; too much silence in worship can make us very uncomfortable. But if you, the worship leader, understand the value of silence, you can help your people to understand and value it too. You can begin to include it in worship by talking about what you are doing and reassuring folks in the beginning; for example, saying, "The silence will last one minute. That will seem like a long time if you are not used to it, but don't worry. I promise not to leave you sitting here with your eyes closed while I go to lunch. If you have to cough, just cough." If you say something about the normal sounds of small children being acceptable, you will not only put the parents at ease, but the whole congregation will be more able to stay in the silence when an infant's sounds interrupt it. You might choose to say something directly to the children about the upcoming period of silence, and they can be encouraged to look at books when the silence becomes hard for them. You can begin with very short silences and slowly lengthen them over time. You might start times of silence with soft, prayerful music, and when people are at ease with that, eliminate the music. Use fewer words in worship; use some silence.

After all, space—emptiness—is not really nothing; it is very full.

Emptiness is what makes a cup useful. It is someone's willingness to empty herself that makes her a compassionate listener. It is when we have space (silence, emptiness, time alone, retreat) that we find ourselves and find renewal. Deepening faith is faith that has more and more space: when we are less filled with our own agendas so we have space for God; when we are less wedded to our own plans so there is more space for other people's needs; when we are less filled with images of God so we leave space for the Great Mystery to emerge in our lives.

I find that another way to offer space is to use poetry as liturgy. To develop this idea in full could fill a book on its own: how to discern good quality poetry, how to read poetry so it communicates, and how to use it as liturgy. Let me just say that if we're trying to use fewer words, poetry offers space. It quickly and concisely presents an image or makes a statement. There is room within the words to move into your own memories or hopes or fears as the poetry evokes them. If good quality poetry is well read (which for most folks takes a lot of practice), it can speak to the hearts and souls of people who are hungry for meaning, for understanding, for courage. I often choose only a section of a poem, because longer ones are hard for people to follow. I receive strong positive responses from parishioners who think they don't like poetry but are moved by the reading in the service. If you would like to consider this, you might begin with some of the poets whose work lends itself to worship, such as those that I often use liturgically, including Wendell Berry, Mary Oliver, Denise Levertov, Rumi, Thich Nhat Hanh, Jane Kenyon, Daniel Ladinsky, and Jan L. Richardson.

In our culture today, what we have plenty of is stimulation. What we need more of is space: silence, emptiness, freedom from noise, from agendas, from consuming, from words. Worship that integrates space in various ways is more likely to take us into the deeper places of our souls.

Practice #7

Create a Safe Intimacy

Sometimes a door opens and a human being
becomes a way for grace to come through.
—*Rumi*[1]

Let's consider another tool for deepening worship: creating a safe intimacy. We'll explore five areas that impact intimacy in worship: the congregation, the leadership style, the environment of worship, boundaries, and integrating visitors and newcomers. We begin with the congregation.

Congregation

There is a vast difference between a congregation and an audience. How well you and your people understand this will shape your church's ministry. The word *congregation* already designates the gathered people as people of faith. We are a congregation only because we are people of faith. The word also implies participation and investment: As members of a congregation, we help our community survive and thrive, we care about its future, and we take some ownership of what happens here. We offer, and expect to offer, skills, money, time, energy, and prayer to the mission and ministry of this community, not all of which will benefit ourselves. We accept, at least in theory, that we in the congregation have a connection with one another.

An *audience,* on the other hand, implies a secular gathering. We are witnesses rather than participants. We are not responsible for what happens at tonight's concert, or for the survival of the orchestra, except perhaps as donors. We do not necessarily have any connection to others in the audience. We paid money (usually) to get something; the focus of the interaction is on what we receive, not what we give.

Since the mid-twentieth century, our society has taught us to be consumers. Unless we are very conscious and intentional, without realizing it, we will approach even our spiritual life and our relationships as consumers: We want a product and so we shop for it, with a mind to having it cost as little as possible. We have no investment in creating that product and no relationship to those who do. When the product no longer satisfies us, we are free to replace it with another. This is the paradigm we support when we blur the distinction between audience and congregation.

You have heard this in your churches. "I'm going to find another church; I don't like the choir here." "This church is always asking me to do something." "I have enough of my own suffering; I don't want to hear about the world's suffering." "This church doesn't meet my needs." These are consumers talking.

There is nothing in the gospel to support the consumer model. Jesus calls us to community-building by way of self-giving love, which requires commitment and sacrifice. The gospel model is about getting ourselves out of center; our needs and preferences are not our reference point. In a marvelous critique of the authority of faith for today's culture, Dale Rosenberger writes, "The self is our default authority setting."[2] This is the way of consumers, but for Christians our authority is elsewhere.

Time spent exploring this issue would be time well spent. Consider the consumer model of our culture. Notice how we live out of that paradigm without awareness; it shapes our choices without our being conscious of it. Read some of the books that critique this contemporary pattern. Can you identify consumer behavior in your church? Do you see it at play in our attitudes toward relationships? Then study the gospel. What kind of model for human community do you find there?

Once this becomes clear to you, it is time to educate your congregation about the difference between congregation and audience, and the impact of those different models. What does it mean to be the church, whose model for human life is so different than the defining paradigm of the culture? Can the older folks articulate how community was different before we evolved into a consumer culture? How does this impact our worship? (Or our relationships? Or our planet?) What is the goal of the spiritual journey? These questions will lead to fruitful discussions in your church and perhaps a deepening understanding of what it means to live the gospel.

In community, we share our struggles and support one another. We use our gifts to help others, and we receive help when we need it. We feel known and cared for; we belong. When people feel part of a community instead of individual consumers, intimacy deepens.

Leadership Style

The personality of the pastor and the history and tradition of the congregation shapes the style of leadership in worship. Some churches have an informal style, some formal. Some leadership styles are pastoral, some more scholarly. None of these are right or wrong; deep worship can emerge from any of them. But whatever your style, if you want to create a safe intimacy in worship, there are some things to consider.

Remember that our culture is much more informal than it was a couple of generations ago. Few congregations expect men to wear suits and ties to every worship, and in some congregations, people wear shorts to church. At one time, no one would have dreamed of addressing the pastor by first name; now it is common, sometimes prefaced with a title such as Father Phil or Pastor Cheryl. Most of our people are comfortable with a little informality in worship.

This may show up during the welcome or the announcements when the pastor or worship leader uses inviting words and a tone of voice that is warm and personal. It may show up when the congregation spontaneously sings "Happy Birthday" to its oldest member. Rites (such as blessing someone who is moving away) and sacraments (such as baptism) may have the actual names inserted in the printed liturgy or even written into hymns for the occasion. The informality is evident when a congregation feels free to laugh out loud.

It is also useful, though, to keep some boundaries around that informality. If we are too informal, our worship can feel like a talk show with the pastor as host. If the informal atmosphere makes it acceptable to whisper and walk around during prayer, we begin to think of God as a warm fuzzy under our control. If we are so informal that we regard the pastor as just one of the gang, we no longer have a spiritual leader.

As worship leaders, if we are clear about the appropriate attitudes for worship, our congregations will be. Informality and reverence are not mutually exclusive. We gather to worship, to stand humbly before God and receive once again God's blessing and God's challenge. We are using tools—words, sacraments, symbols—that have been instruments for God's work for two thousand years and more; the only proper approach to that is awe, humility, and reverence.

A skilled and centered worship leader can lead worship in such a way that a congregation is laughing together at one moment, completely silent at another, and somber with confession in yet another part of the service. A leader can speak personally in some parts of the service, acknowledging by name Stu and Della's sixty-fifth anniversary, Randy's week at church camp, and Alice and Terry's adoption of their son; at another point in the service, the leader reads the ancient and formal words of the faith, true in every time and place, universal as well as personal. There is room for both informality and reverence.

It is useful to watch your own style and your congregation's comfort level with different degrees of casualness or formality. Perhaps you could ask some members of the congregation to reflect on that with you. Are you creating the intimacy that helps to build community and open people to faith? Some informality will foster that; too much informality will destroy it.

Another leadership issue that determines how deep your worship can be is how you see your role in the congregation. How does your congregation perceive your role? We discussed this in Practice #1. Congregations, influenced by the models that they know, will try to put you in roles such as business administrator, therapist, good buddy, or professional organizer and fund-raiser. When that happens, a corporate model or a therapeutic model shapes worship, and the gospel takes on no more significance than a logo.

Your role is to be a spiritual leader. Your role is pastoral and prophetic. Your role is to be a person of prayer, teaching others how to be people of prayer. Yours is a servant leadership. You represent a very particular set of values and a very particular worldview. This is a role of great intimacy: You must be intimate with God and with sacred scripture, and with our tradition. You will be intimate with human evil and human triumph. You will be intimate with the people of your congregation, invited into their homes in times of deepest grief and greatest celebration. But it is an intimacy with boundaries: You are not God's peer. You are not buddies with your congregation. Your ethical behavior must be beyond question.

Sometimes as pastors, we are afraid to claim the role of spiritual leader. Isn't it presumptuous? Or arrogant? And what about all the clergy who abuse that role? Isn't it dangerous to think the pastor is holier than her people?

You are a spiritual leader not because you are holier than your people (you're not), but because you are set apart so God can use you in a specific way. You are a person of prayer not because you know how to pray better than your people, but because you need to be a person of prayer to do the work you are called to do. When you are clear about this and live out this role faithfully, the worship in your congregation will inevitably lead the people deeper into their lives and faith.

Environment of Worship

Intimacy is profoundly affected by the environment of worship. Our ideas of what should happen in worship change over time, and so our ideas of worship space change too. If you look at books about contemporary church architecture, you will see how many of the sanctuary designs foster an intimacy (between pastor and people; between members of the Body) that did not seem so important to us in the past.

Imagine two different sanctuaries, with about one hundred people in each. In one, worship is in the round. Chairs are arranged in a circle, with an altar/communion table in the center. The worship leader often walks around the inside of the circle and sits in the circle like everyone else. This makes the worship space very intimate. In the other church, the pews are arranged in straight rows. Perhaps the church is larger than the current congregation, and so the people are widely scattered over a large space. The pastor is probably removed from the rows of people, sometimes by a considerable distance. This setting makes it harder for connections to happen. These two different images of worship space show how much the environment of worship can determine the level of intimacy. When we worship in a circle, the environment helps create community. When we worship in rows, the environment seems to define the people as audience, and creating intimacy is much harder.

That does not mean, however, that worshiping in the round is the only way or the best way. It can be intimidating to visitors, and if you are not careful, it can make it more difficult for some people to hear well. Some congregations prefer the formality to which traditional worship space lends itself. You can build a safe and appropriate intimacy in any building (in some more easily than others) if you are mindful of your purpose: making the architecture serve the gospel. Regardless of your congregation's building or preferences, if you hope to foster a safe and appropriate intimacy that can lead worshipers more deeply into community, you will want to consider the environment of your space. Look with me at some ways we might arrange a sanctuary. Imagine how the intimacy feels in each; think about how much each space encourages connection—between pastor and people, between people and the Word, between and among worshipers. We'll consider worship in the round, worship in rows, and variations of each.

I think worshiping in the round is a wonderful way to make worship deeper and community stronger. It is not for everyone, but I'd like to begin here and encourage you to think about this possibility. I have worshiped in the round in a small congregation and a large one; so size does not necessarily determine whether this option might work for you. Creating a circle is easiest, obviously, if you use chairs instead of pews. If you decide to try this, make concentric circles so there are at least two rows of chairs; visitors will feel safer in the second row, and smaller concentric circles are more intimate than one very large one. Leave small aisles in several places in the circle so people have easy access to the chairs. Be mindful of how close you position the chairs to the center where the table or the pastor is; too close feels uncomfortable and too far away loses the intimacy the circle tries to create. Modify the circle by creating a semicircle, with the altar/table, pulpit, and worship leader not in the center of the circle but in the open part of the semicircle. This reduces intimacy somewhat but is still more intimate than rows.

If, like most churches, you have beautiful pews bolted in rows, you may still be able to alter the environment if you want to—and this will be a hot issue, so make any such plans very slowly and with the congregation's input. When it is time for remodeling, you can replace the pews with chairs so you can change the environment of the sanctuary as needed. Use the pews as wonderful benches in hallways and fellowship rooms, or sell them to raise money for a project or mission for which the church has a passion.

If you want to keep the pews, unbolt them and arrange them in a circle of sorts: Even though the pews are long and straight, it is usually possible to set them on a diagonal in three or four sections around a center, so it creates the effect of a circle. Or follow the custom of old monasteries, which had the monks or nuns sit in straight rows but facing one another instead of facing forward; this builds the sense of community too. The sanctuary could have two sections facing each other or four sections facing a common center. Or move the pews so that instead of straight forward-facing rows on each side of a center aisle, there are diagonal rows on each side of the aisle; while the pews still partially face forward, they are also open more to the other worshipers, thus enhancing the sense of community.

If you decide to move the table, baptismal font, pulpit, and worship leaders to the center, you may, if you have a traditional church, have the chancel area left over. I have been in several churches that creatively solved this problem: Some use that space for art that pertains to the theme of the day or season, and the effect is to take the importance and possibilities of art in worship more seriously. Some churches use this space for abundant live plants (if light permits), which add a calming and healing energy to the worship space. Although intimacy is enhanced when all worship leaders, including musicians, are in—or as near as possible to—the circle with the rest of the congregation, the chancel area could be a place for a piano or bell choir tables if necessary. And if your church uses media, this is a good space for the screen; in that case, of course, do not create a complete circle because some people will not be able to see the screen; a semicircle or diagonal rows will work.

If you do not want to change your sanctuary, there are still ways to alter the environment a bit, thus fostering safe intimacy. The pastor can move out from behind the pulpit or move the pulpit closer to the congregation. The worship leaders can move into the church aisles to read the scripture, offer prayer, or make announcements. You can move the altar or communion table forward so that instead of being at the far end of the chancel, it is near the first row of pews. Or keep the beautiful altar that has been in your church for more than one hundred years in the chancel, and add a communion table nearer to the congregation.

Be creative with your space, and often even a small change can make a big difference in the feeling of community. As you envision possibilities, two questions can guide you: How can you reduce the distance between the worship leader (and the worship furnishings such as the pulpit, font, or table) and the congregation? And how can you open the congregation so the people see and feel connected to one another? Creating safe intimacy is one way to help deepen your worship.

Boundaries

Our society has become very casual and informal; our talk shows make public bleeding seem like a valuable form of communication; and many of the people in our congregations did not grow up in church. And so it is sometimes necessary to help people know what is appropriate for public worship. When there are no boundaries, it may seem that we are fostering intimacy, but it is not a safe intimacy.

A full discussion of clergy sexual ethics is outside the scope of this book, but we must at least name this most important of all boundaries in church; sexual liaisons between pastor and parishioner are forbidden. As clergy know, it is not enough to avoid inappropriate intimacy; we must avoid even the appearance of it. Both clergy and congregation should be well educated about this issue.

There is also much attention today on creating safe space for children and all who come to the church. Some insist that two adults should always be present with any child; some say that a pastor must never counsel a congregant behind closed doors or hug parishioners. It is vital that your community consider these issues and find ways to create safe space while still maintaining the ministry of hospitality to which the church is called.

Let's look at some other boundaries as they affect worship. I was a part of a church that had a strong sense of community. We valued our time of joys and concerns when people shared what was on their hearts, but when one worshiper, sobbing, described his recent assault in detail, and another went on for several minutes about her spouse's infidelity, we decided that we had to set some limits. We appreciated our community's tradition of openness and honesty, but felt details weren't appropriate in public worship. We did not name any issue taboo, but we tried to educate people about the words they chose and the time and intensity they used to share their concerns. We never singled out one individual to criticize, in public or private, what they chose to share, but sometimes when the community gathered (before worship or at congregational and committee meetings), we talked about why some details were not appropriate for worship, inviting folks to share their full stories in the pastor's office or with individuals during fellowship time. We wanted worship that was honest; we had seen too many churches that expected people to leave their pain at the door, but we also thought that public worship should not instill fear in the children or horrify someone's visiting grandmother. Without any boundaries, the community is not a safe place.

A similar issue can arise when people ask for prayer for someone who is ill. All of the medical details are not necessary or appropriate in worship. This became very clear to our church one Sunday. Don wanted the congregation to pray for his nephew Ken who had surgery and was experiencing life-threatening complications. Because of the fear and anxiety he felt for Ken, Don wanted to pour out the whole painful story. But he refrained, simply asking for prayers for Ken's healing. The next person to speak was Marcia, who requested prayers for herself: The following day she was facing the same surgery that Ken had undergone. Don was so grateful that he had skipped the alarming details of Ken's complications, details that would have been frightening for Marcia to hear the day before her surgery.

Worship is not a support group or a twelve-step meeting or a talk show. Though it is a place to bring our problems, the focus is not on our problems, but on God. When the emotion gets too raw or the language too graphic, people will quickly distance themselves, and worship ceases to be safe space.

There are few hard and fast rules about boundaries; a formal congregation that has worshiped in a high church style for 125 years will have very different ideas of what's appropriate than a new storefront church that attracts mostly young people who feel marginalized. I encourage worship leaders to be clear about the differences between worship and other forms of public gatherings. The intimacy in worship needs to be genuine, but also safe.

Church etiquette is about boundaries too. As our culture changes and more and more people have not grown up in a church, well-meaning folks may be oblivious to some of these concerns. A little gentle education may be in order; for example, "In church, we don't walk or talk during prayer." "We don't eat or drink (unless medication makes water necessary) through the service." "We don't answer cell phones (or permit them to ring) during worship." Some emerging churches who reach out to young unchurched folks purposely create a familiar atmosphere that allows for sipping coffee or talking during the service, but this will not foster spiritual depth. Some restraints are in order for the sake of depth and also because a church community is a great place to practice what our culture never teaches: It's not all about me!

Some behaviors that might normally be regarded as disruptive can still be appropriate. The occasional wiggles and murmurings of children are definitely a part of the intimacy of worship. The words or movement of a person with disabilities may be a little distracting, but if they are beyond that person's ability to control, then they become part of the intimacy of the family at worship. Accepting people the way they are makes intimate worship safe for them. Educating people about appropriate boundaries makes intimate worship safe for others.

Integrating Visitors and Newcomers

After nearly twenty-five years in the pulpit, I suddenly found myself sitting in the pews. I was a newcomer, and not just at one church but at the many churches I visited in several parts of the country. In most of those churches, people rarely spoke to me. I learned quickly how uncomfortable it can be to be a visitor in worship.

Welcoming the stranger is a very important ministry, and there are many resources to help you do it well. I know that when we feel awkward or uncomfortable, when we feel overlooked or left out, we do not move into a deeper interior space of prayer; we are not able to rest in God; we cannot risk an open heart. So crafting deep worship means making the stranger feel at home. Some of you already do that very well, but if you are still working on it, here are a few ideas. This is by no means an exhaustive list, but it is enough to get you started or to give you food for discussion within your community.

Maybe your church could have a person or committee who is responsible for greeting newcomers, following up with them after their visit, inviting them to church events, and introducing them to other people. Welcoming newcomers is the responsibility of the whole congregation, of course, but one person or committee could be designated to help that happen.

When Ruth is a greeter, she chats warmly with Paul, a visitor. She specifically introduces Paul to Enid, asking Enid to help Paul find a place to sit. Enid talks briefly with Paul, then walks him to a seat, and introduces him to Tim, who is sitting nearby. Each person takes the responsibility of seeing that Paul is always in good hands.

When a visitor walks into your church, is it clear where the restrooms are? Could he find the nursery? Does she know to pick up a hymnal or bulletin from the table at the door of the sanctuary? How will they know whether they or their children are welcome to share in communion?

Suppose Amy has come to the church several times and indicated an interest in continuing. You might assign Jo as Amy's "guardian angel." Jo agrees to sit with Amy for a few weeks until she gets acquainted, to offer her a ride to the mid-week Lenten worship, and to explain the upcoming Holy Week traditions. Amy has someone to call on when she wonders if she'll be welcome at the dinner announced in the bulletin or if she has to register to join in the Habitat project.

Some churches have occasional gatherings for newcomers at the pastor's home. This is not a class for prospective members, but just an opportunity for the pastor and new folks to get acquainted, more in the fashion of an open house than a meeting. A few church members might be there too, so newcomers can connect a few more names and faces.

When I write a welcome note to visitors, instead of sending a typed letter on church letterhead, I write my note by hand on attractive stationery or note cards. I am amazed at the positive response this brings over and over again. Many folks rarely get personal letters anymore. I find that people receive this simple gesture as a gift.

If everyone in the church sings the prayer response by heart, that act fosters intimacy, but it leaves the newcomer painfully on the outside. If you announce that Bible study will be at Anita's house, everyone will feel invited except visitors who have no idea who Anita is, much less where she lives. There are many examples like this, where familiarity builds the intimacy of the community but leaves out the folks who stand at the edge of the circle. You need to find the balance that will allow the congregation to be intimate but not exclusive.

Congregation, leadership style, environment of worship space, boundaries, integrating visitors and newcomers—these are areas that help to determine the intimacy of worship. They merit your attention. When there is a safe and appropriate intimacy in worship, people let their defenses down, and that is when they can rest in the deeper places where Spirit moves.

Practice #8
Make Worship Inclusive

To love someone is not first of all to do things for them,
but to reveal to them their beauty and value.
—*Jean Vanier*[1]

These days there is a lot of talk about inclusion. That is not new, however. Jesus always included those his society marginalized: the woman at the well, Matthew the tax collector, the poor, the lepers, the woman about to be stoned, the children. He always invited people back into community. If we are going to follow Jesus, we will be called, over and over, to make room for people we might prefer to avoid. And if we are concerned with crafting our worship so it offers people the opportunity to go deeper, then we must consider this issue. When we feel included, we forget about ourselves and are free to focus on God or a person in need. The moment we feel left out, we jerk back into our heads, into our thinking, critiquing selves. When that happens, we lose the capacity to enter the spaces of deep prayer, awe, and self-forgetfulness. Deep worship must be inclusive worship.

In this chapter, I name some things that make worship inclusive. I will not offer an in-depth discussion of any of these issues, because there are many resources available for that. My focus is on making worship deeper: How do we include people and ideas in such a way that worshipers feel free to move more deeply into their true selves, into community, or into God? This chapter is really about the ancient virtue of hospitality, the practice of including the guest in the very best of what we ourselves have received.[2] So how do we make people feel welcome? What allows people to feel that they belong? How do we model in our community the radical love of God? Let's begin with the children.

Including Children

I hope that in your church the children are part of the worshiping community each week. Sunday School will never give them the same essential gifts that come from standing in the midst of the singing, praying community, taking in how adults worship and pray. This time is also a good opportunity for children to begin building relationships with their pastor. Many churches find it works well to have the children in worship for the first few minutes and then leave the sanctuary to go to their classes. In other communities, the children are in worship the whole hour. In either case, how do we authentically include them?

If you call the children forward for a story or conversation, sit on their level; don't stand, towering over them. Speak at their level too; children relate to concrete stories and activities, not abstract theological concepts. In your conversation, be focused, be brief, and be simple. Remember that children have short attention spans. Make this time participatory: Engage the children by using props, asking questions, or inviting them to do something. These are the simplest of ground rules, yet I have been to many churches that don't follow them: The pastor stands above the children, offering them a monologue about something the young ones don't begin to understand, much less care about. The children's boredom is obvious. They may be sitting on the chancel steps, but they are not really being included.

Some churches make sure the children are included in worship by offering each child a children's bulletin, a worship bag filled with books, paper, and crayons, or a table of quiet games, puzzles, and markers in the back corner of the sanctuary. I have successfully used all these methods. If you make worship bags, someone will need to renew the bags each week, removing old paper and broken crayons and changing the contents now and then. If you put a quiet table in the sanctuary, be sure to instruct a parent to accompany each child, or arrange for an adult to sit at the table. And remember to show visitors that these options are available.

If your church is unable to provide Sunday School for children, or during the summer when Sunday School takes a break, you can make worship intergenerational—child friendly—once a month or several times throughout the year. This worked very well in churches I have served. The service and even the bulletin had fewer and simpler words. We chose easy hymns appropriate for children. The scripture was proclaimed in a skit, puppet show, or story. We built the service around one theme or story—one of the stories by or about Jesus or a contemporary story that portrays a faith value, or a theme such as friendship, honesty, God's love, creation. The service was shorter than usual, only about forty-five minutes. We gave a special name to these Sundays and publicized them well so adults were prepared for something different and so the children could anticipate something special. They turned into very creative services—and yet were not so unusual as to lose the sense that we were a worshiping community with certain practices and traditions to honor. We found that adults enjoyed these services too, because making them simple did not mean making them trite.

If you want children to feel included in worship, you might use more visual signs in the sanctuary and in the bulletin. Must you be able to read to participate in worship, or are there parts in the order of worship that are designated in the bulletin by an image? Have some simple songs or responses that the congregation (including the children) learn by heart so no reading is required. Worship can occasionally include movement or actions with simple songs or a body prayer—a prayer with movement.

Do the children get to light the candles, hold the chalice during communion, sing in a choir, or offer a reader's theater? If you practice the passing of the peace, watch to see if adults greet the children or if they just look over the children and greet other adults; you might need to do some work on this one.

At my church when a child is baptized, we invite not only the child's family, but all of the church's children to gather around the baptismal font. We invite them to participate in simple ways, such as holding out their hands toward the child being baptized in the sign of blessing, or repeating some words of blessing after the pastor, or forming a circle around the child and his or her family as a sign that we are encircling them in our love and care. If your church serves communion to children, does the server bend (if she is able) to the child's level? What other ways does your church include or fail to include the children?

Including Elders and Youth

I loved the occasional Sundays when I could worship with my father. I stood next to him and heard his voice blending with mine as we said the Lord's Prayer. I listened to his voice as he sang the beloved hymns that he had sung pretty much every Sunday for ninety years. One particular Sunday, all of the hymns were contemporary and new to the congregation, printed on inserts. My father tried the first hymn, but finding it hard to keep up with music he didn't know, he soon dropped out. The other hymns were unfamiliar too; he got lost and didn't sing any of them. I missed blending my voice with his and felt sad. But most of all I felt angry. Dad had been excluded from an essential form of worship. The issue was not the introduction of a new hymn; it was the introduction of three new hymns at once, so that those who do not quickly pick up new music were left out of *all* the music that day.

As worship leader, if you want to include the elders, you must honor tradition. That does not mean you don't bring change; if you don't use contemporary forms of worship, you will exclude the youth. But introduce new music or practices slowly, and surround the new parts of worship with what is familiar. It is not important (or possible) to please everyone—it is essential to consider everyone.

To help elders feel included, you might draw some of your sermon illustrations from earlier decades. Be attentive to the need for some large-print bulletins and hymnals and a good sound system. If you have movement during the service (coming forward for communion, for instance), do you allow time for those who walk at a slower pace? When you lift up the saints of our tradition, include those who lived well into old age.

On the other hand, are all of your sermon illustrations drawn from "ancient history"? You want the youth to feel welcome as well. To make that happen, use some contemporary music, and share readings and quotes from modern authors and current media. You'll want at least some parts of the service to be lively and energetic. How old is your hymnal? Do you use instruments other than an organ?

These are the kinds of issues that fuel the infamous worship wars, and though the divide is often made along generational lines, it is certainly not always; people don't fit so easily into boxes. It is important to look at your worship through the eyes of your elders and of your youth to see who is overlooked, who feels excluded. However, when worship takes us deeper, we move beyond the worship wars. If worship helps us make connections with our true selves and with the community and with God, if worship moves us from our heads to our hearts, we respond with gratitude instead of criticism. Perhaps when we fight over which music to use in church, what we are really struggling with is our relentless hunger.

Worship is not about giving everyone what they want—the consumer model. Even so, if we want our worship to be inclusive, which it must be if we want to feel free and safe enough to be self-forgetful, then as we plan worship, we must recognize that different generations have different reference points and probably different expectations about worship. How are your elders and your youth feeling dismissed? How are they feeling included?

Including People Who Look Different than We Do

We want to love our neighbor and see the face of Christ in each person we meet. We want to. But to live in community with people who are different is sometimes scary and always hard work. If we commit to being a church of radical welcome, where do we begin? What must we consider if we want to offer hospitality and welcome to those of various racial and ethnic backgrounds?

Some passages in our gospel are very anti-Semitic. These need to be read with some caution or adjustment, or you must address their inherent bias in the homily. If you are not already aware of this issue, you need to educate yourself about it.

If all of the cartoons in the newsletter, illustrations in the sermon, and posters on the bulletin boards portray people just like you, people of different races, classes, economic levels, or ethnic groups will feel invisible—and rightly so. Be attentive to these unspoken messages.

Consider which historical figures you lift up as saints and heroes and holy people; are they all white Western Christians? Do the necessary research to broaden your role models.

In your language, be careful not to always equate black with evil and white with good. Are you mindful of the inherent racism in words such as blacklist, black magic, black market?

Many of us were shaped by a Christian tradition that comes from Western Europe. Today vibrant Christianity comes out of Africa and Asia. Inclusive worship might draw some music, prayers, and readings from those sources.

Use artwork from different cultures. Books and online resources offer Christian art from all parts of the world. It can have a significant impact on worshipers because it is different from what we are used to and moves us out of the box, opening us to new insights and interpretations.

If you live near a worshiping community different from your own, visiting them or arranging a combined choir or a pulpit exchange can be a wonderful experience. If your church comes from a Western European heritage, see if there is a Chinese church in your area, or a traditional black church, or an Eastern Orthodox church, and ask if you can worship with them some Sunday. Arrange to visit a mosque or a synagogue. Perhaps someone from the host church can visit with you to teach you about their tradition and answer your questions.

You may live in a situation that is very homogeneous (though fewer and fewer of us do). It is still important that our worship express racial and ethnic diversity. How else will our hearts grow big enough to welcome the stranger? How else will we recognize that everyone on the planet is our neighbor, whom we are commanded to love? How else will our worship make connections to the nightly news?

Including People of Differing Sexual Orientations

I am painfully aware that this is the hot issue in today's church. If you talk about this in your church—and I strongly urge you to do so— be gentle and respectful. Self-righteousness is not helpful. If your community decides to make your worship inclusive of gay and lesbian people, here are some ways to do that:

Say the words out loud in worship, and print them in liturgies: words such as *gay, lesbian, bisexual, transgendered,* and *glbt* (a common abbreviation). If you mean to be welcoming but never name these words, remember that in this case, silence screams.

Vary the images of family that you use in sermon illustrations and children's stories: Our culture includes a great diversity of family structure. Use the words *spouse* or *partner* as well as the words *husband* and *wife.* Talk about *covenant unions* as well as *weddings.*

Read the liberation texts in the Bible—there are many. You might begin with Acts 8:26–40 and Acts 10. Most people have only heard the texts of terror that seem to condemn gay and lesbian people. Help people to see how Jesus constantly included the marginalized.

Make connections between the biblical story and gay experience, comparing, for instance, the Hebrews' exodus from oppression to freedom with the personal journey of coming out and the public journey toward justice.

Use liturgy that acknowledges oppression and injustice of all kinds. Sing hymns that wrestle with oppression, liberation, and justice. You will find powerful images in contemporary music and also in many old gospel hymns.

Be mindful of the church's history toward glbt people, and do not assume that gay worshipers will equate *church* with words like *good* or *safe*.

Use words with sensitivity. *Sin* has a different meaning to those who have been told that their essential being is sin; *pride* has one meaning in the Bible (arrogance, relying on self instead of God) and quite another meaning for modern oppressed people (self-acceptance of one's inherent worth). Being described as a *homosexual* feels different than being described as a *gay man* or *lesbian*. It can be helpful to create a safe space for people to talk about these issues together: Which words are trigger words for you and why? What words seem neutral to one group of people but are considered demeaning by another group? Can you relate your experience in such a way that others will understand why a certain word is offensive to you?

Speak generously of God's unconditional love.

Remember that there is great power in what comes from the pulpit. Don't set up discussions of this topic in your adult education class and yet in worship, act like the issue doesn't exist. In fact, remember that this isn't an *issue* we are talking about but *human beings*. If lesbians and gays come to your church, they will be asking, "Does Jesus have room for me?" They will hear the answer to that question in your worship.

Including Both Women and Men

This issue has been with us for a long time, but it is still trouble-some. If you want inclusive worship, if you want worship that does not permit feelings of exclusion to get in the way of deepening faith, look at the language of your hymns, your sermons, your liturgies, your church school curriculum.

There is no excuse for using male language for humans; too many options exist and are very common. It is not that difficult to learn to say *humankind* instead of *mankind, firefighter* instead of *fireman, all people* instead of *all men*. Inclusive language hymnals are widely available now, and The New Revised Standard Version Bible is one respected translation that makes human language inclusive.

God language is much more sensitive. It is never wrong to address God in one way; but it is seriously limiting to address God in *only* one way. Leave God the Father as an honored and worthy way to name the Holy, but start adding names; the Bible itself gives many examples, including feminine ones. God is also Mother, Source, Beloved, Creator; the names are infinite.

Changing the words of much-loved hymns can be difficult, and of course, there are sometimes copyright issues. Talk about why you want to change "Rise Up, O Men of God" to "Rise Up, O Saints of God." Compromise by changing one hymn but not the others on a Sunday morning. Avoid changing the most beloved hymns on the high holy days: Altering the words to "Silent Night" on Christmas Eve will probably not deepen your worship!

Does the congregation hear both male and female voices in worship leadership? Are the stories of women in the Bible well represented in worship? (You may have to alter or add to lectionary readings to accomplish this.) Do you lift up both male and female saints and holy people?

What images of *boys* and *girls* do the children receive in Sunday

School? If you want your church to be inclusive, don't make assumptions based on gender! Our church once hosted an ecumenical lunch for clergy. One of our guests complimented the ladies on the gourmet meal and the beautifully appointed tables. We took great pleasure in introducing Peter, our cook, and Byron, our table decorator!

Including People of Differing Abilities

Besides issues of your building's accessibility, there are other ways to say *welcome* to people with disabilities. Don't be shy about educating your congregation on these issues. Remember that people with disabilities are people first; the disability is only part of who they are.

Do you have a few large-print bulletins and hymnals?

Have you found ways to make the service comfortable for people with some hearing impairment? Do you know for sure if such people can hear all of worship? I was in ministry for years before I learned that when telling a powerful story during a sermon, my voice became very soft as I spoke the dramatic ending, and therefore, some people never heard the end of the story. I was embarrassed, but also very grateful when a church member pointed this out to me.

Make room for wheelchairs in the body of the congregation instead of only in the aisle or at the back of the sanctuary. When people talk to someone in a wheelchair, do they sit or kneel so they do not tower over the chair-bound person?

Does your church offer rides to people who could not otherwise get to church?

People with disabilities could be in your choir or on some committees even though their contributions may, depending on the disability, be limited. In one church I served, someone thought to ask Jody if she'd like to serve on the worship committee. She was delighted to be asked and said yes. Because of her disability, Jody was not always able to participate fully in discussions, but she contributed beautifully to the committee's prayer and community-building.

Consider offering the worship service, or even just one prayer, in sign language.

In pictures of children in Sunday School curriculum, posters of families on bulletin boards, images of people circling the globe on the worship bulletin, be sure there are people in wheelchairs or with service dogs.

If your worship invites movement (from standing to simple liturgical dance), remember to be sensitive to people who are unable to move that way. Plan movement so that everyone can participate somehow, regardless of abilities.

It is not a disability but our failure to be sensitive to that disability that becomes an obstacle to moving into a deeper place in worship.

Including Saints and Holy Ones

Our culture offers us more stars than saints. We can name many famous people, but few holy ones—not because there are no holy ones, but because there aren't many TV shows about them. If you want to create worship that invites people deeper, you need to include the saints and holy ones. These are the pioneers of our faith. These are the ones who show us the full purpose and potential of a human being. These are the people who model for us what it is to live like Christ. These are our companions on the journey, the great cloud of witnesses that the writer of Hebrews talks about (Hebrews 12:1). If we don't include them in our worship (and Christian education), then we are telling our folks that the popular stars of our culture are better models than the godly saints of our faith. Here are a few ways to include the saints and holy ones in worship:

Build a service around Teresa of Avila, St. Francis, Julian of Norwich, or the many other saints of our Christian tradition. Tell the stories of their lives, use their own words as liturgy, make connections between their lives and work and modern concerns and issues.

Share the stories of more obscure often-unnamed biblical women.

Lift up the Christlike people who have lived in our lifetimes, such as Thomas Merton, Mother Teresa, Brother Roger of Taizé, Jean Vanier, Dorothy Day, Oscar Romero. Include the holy people of other traditions and cultures like Gandhi, Thich Nhat Hanh, the Dalai Lama.

Plan a series during Lent (martyrs for justice) or Advent (people who helped birth God into the world), including the story and wisdom of a different person each week of the season. Show a feature film or documentary about that person the same week you highlight him in worship or study her in Sunday School.

Focus on one issue, and lift up one of our saints and holy ones whose wisdom informs that issue; for instance, let St. Francis help you look at issues of environment; Hildegard of Bingen, issues about women's roles; Martin Luther King Jr. or the Islamic Badshah Khan[3] about non-violence; the Desert Mothers and Fathers for learning about prayer.

Use quotes from our faith heroes as worship liturgy, even when they are not included in the service in other ways. Be sure to credit that quote. Use their stories and words in sermons.

Teach the children about these holy people. Bring the saints to life: Use skits, puppet shows, and stories to make the great ones of our faith familiar and trusted companions to our children.

Maybe your efforts need to begin with yourself: How well do you know this great cloud of witnesses that surrounds you? Make their acquaintance; they are marvelous company.

Including People from Other Nations

Making worship inclusive leads us to broaden our awareness of others. It is so easy for us to become very parochial. God's love embraces all the peoples of the earth, and Christianity is most vibrant today in cultures very different from our own. The church at worship is the church universal. Here are some ways to open our worship to the peoples and places of God's community:

Use prayers from other nations. Be sure that the bulletin names the country from which they come. The English translation of the Maori version of the Lord's Prayer[4] is beautiful and opens us to a broader understanding of this prayer.

When using prayers or readings from other parts of the world, occasionally use some of the original images, even if they do not fit our culture; such images bring our sisters and brothers around the world into our presence and prayers. In this prayer from West Africa, for instance, the image of cassava (an edible root plant) brings the West Africans into our hearts even as their prayer of thanksgiving speaks for us as well:

> Lord of lords, Creator of all things ...
> The rain watered the earth,
> the sun drew cassava and corn out of the clay.
> Your mercy showered blessing after blessing
> over our lands.[5]

Learn a few hymns or chants in another language. Many newer hymnals include some of these, especially in Spanish. Read a little about how this is handled in the Taizé community.[6] Taizé music is familiar to many churches, and often the introductions in their songbooks will encourage you to sing the chants in the original language. Practice and reassure people that speaking the words correctly is not nearly as important as participating.

Consider highlighting one country or people each week or each month. You could use a prayer or reading from that culture, lift up in prayer some of the current concerns of the people of that nation, use a picture from that place for your bulletin cover, sing a hymn common in that country or sung in its language.

Use art from other nations as your bulletin covers and your sanctuary decorations. Use such art as an object for meditation.

Consider hanging a map of the world in the sanctuary. If you do this, you might consider the Peters Projection Map,[7] which attempts to correct the great inaccuracies present in our familiar maps, inaccuracies that come from a bias toward Western industrialized nations. You might build a sermon around the differences between the maps and the bias and injustice built into our familiar maps.

Display a large map in the sanctuary, perhaps on World Communion Sunday, and invite people to put a pin in the country from which their ancestors come, a city with which they have some significant connection, or a region they feel moved to keep in prayer for the next week.

If your tradition allows for this, invite people to bring bread from other cultures (naan, tortillas, rye bread, rice cakes, and so on) for communion; again, World Communion Sunday is a good time to do this. Use communion liturgy that lifts up different breads and the cultures and peoples they represent.

You can bring other nations and cultures into your worship in so many ways. Because our world is very small, our worship must be very large.

Including Other Faith Traditions

This may be a new idea for you. We certainly live in a global village now, and the people in our congregations are exposed, on the Internet, in their book clubs, and maybe in their neighborhoods, to the words, people, and practices of other faiths. I understand the major and ancient world faith traditions, including the faiths of many indigenous people, to be carriers of the greatest wisdom of the human species. I do not underestimate the profound differences in rituals and worldviews between these diverse faiths, but I do believe that in their deepest essence, they all speak a language of compassion, justice, peace, self-giving, and humility. Sometimes hearing another way of expressing a truth that we hold as Christians can bring new life and fresh insights into our own familiar words. And so I sometimes use words from other faiths in Christian worship. If you don't feel free to do this in your worship service, you might try it at prayer services, committee meetings, or church programs.

This opens some issues, of course. Some Christians believe that other faiths are inferior to Christianity, or that, as some would say, only Christians are saved. At the other extreme are people who are so open to borrowing from other faiths that their commitment to their own faith is compromised. Some people create their own religion, putting together practices and insights borrowed from many places. Such a personalized faith rarely contains the deep challenges to our ego that an ancient wisdom tradition offers, and it puts the human in the position of being the ultimate authority: a popular but dangerous place to be.

There is also a controversy about using the words of other faiths. Some see it as exploitive, as appropriation, as an act of dishonoring or of injustice. So far, I have not shared that view. The Prayer of St. Francis is Christian, but it is known and loved and used by people of any faith and no apparent faith, because its truths are universal. Some of the teachings in any wisdom tradition are universal and belong to us all. If you do choose to use them, and there are books that offer such resources, it is essential that you credit the faith from which the reading or prayer practice comes and that it is used with respect. I have found this to be a wonderful way to live out the solidarity that we sing about, to include other peoples in our awareness and in our prayers, to reduce the prejudice that people might have about other faiths, and to open people to new ways of understanding our own prayers and teachings.

When I plan worship, I may use a reading from the sacred scripture or devotional work of another faith tradition as a prayer, litany, or call to worship. Canticles of praise or prayers of confession are universal, are they not? Once I built a service around the Great Commandment in Matthew 22:37–39. The liturgy was from some of the world's sacred scriptures (the Koran, the Torah, the Sutta Nipata, the Upanishads, the Tao Te Ching, the Bible); in some way, each selection presented the same truth (love God with all your heart, soul, and mind; and love your neighbor as yourself) as our Great Commandment. In this case, I ignored my usual rule, "use fewer words," and printed the entire liturgy in the bulletin, identifying the scripture and faith from which each came. People appreciated this small exposure to other sacred scriptures, and seeing the universality of this wisdom brought our own words of scripture to life for them. One Pentecost I did something similar, building the service around the theme of spiritual practices such as prayer, fasting, nonviolent action, compassion, and justice for the oppressed—practices valued in our Christianity that are also essential to other world religions.

We can include other Christian traditions as well. There is often as much ignorance and prejudice about other Christian faiths as about other world faiths. One Sunday I planned a worship service that lifted up the great diversity within Christianity. We named some of the different traditions, sang hymns and spoke prayers that came from various denominations, and lifted up the gifts that different Christian religions offer to the whole church.

We live in a very small world. It is also a world in which there is much religious violence. I prefer to honor other traditions and help people to regard them without fear, ignorance, or arrogance. I find that occasionally including some wisdom from different faith traditions, Christian and non-Christian, helps my congregations move more deeply into our own faith traditions.

Including Politics, Peace, and Justice

The deeper we go in prayer and faith, the more we connect to the world. The inner leads us to the outer. God calls us to both places. Worship should always hold a connection to the nightly news.

If your congregation is not used to including awareness of or prayers for world events in worship, begin with issues that are not controversial: Talk about war refugees instead of the administration's war policies or hunger and homelessness instead of abortion and gay marriage. More controversial issues can come later.

Preach the gospel. Help the people see how Jesus challenged the powerful, defied the community-destroying purity codes, and welcomed the marginalized. Show your congregation how much both testaments in the Bible are about politics, struggles about who has the power and controls the resources. Make connections between the way of Jesus (or the words of the Hebrew prophets) and the events in our newspaper.

Some congregations may help those who fall through the cracks in the system; they might feed the hungry. Other communities may choose to help change the system; they might work to eliminate some of the causes of hunger and homelessness. In any case, your worship should lead your community into the world and its needs.

Worship is not an escape from the world, but at the same time, worship is not a political rally with a veneer of religious language. Be clear that worship is first about God. Look at your own theology and perhaps your own fear or despair. Does your worship mirror the angst of the culture or offer the strength, hope, and joy of the gospel? Contemporary theologian and author Walter Wink shows us that although the New Testament is very realistic about the evil and horrors and threats from the powers of the world, it is totally free of gloom. There is no despair anywhere in the gospels and epistles, no quailing before the powers—only the absolute certainty of God's ultimate victory.[8] Our worship needs to be realistic about the world's problems but firmly grounded in the gospel's trust.

In this chapter, we discussed many possibilities for inclusion or exclusion, but we have only touched the surface of these issues because the main focus of this book lies elsewhere. And we left out things we could have included, such as inclusion of people with mental illness and sensitivity to abuse survivors. But I've said enough, I hope, to convince you that deep worship is inclusive worship, because when we feel unsafe or unwelcome, we stay in our heads with our defenses, and if we feel invisible, we don't move into self-forgetfulness.

In your sincere efforts to be inclusive, don't resort to the lowest common denominator. I once worked with a church that was so committed to welcoming everyone, they were afraid to take a stand on anything, including the gospel of Jesus Christ. That is not the point. I also want to emphasize that in discussing inclusion, I am talking about welcome and hospitality, not about rights. I appreciate Dale Rosenberger's distinction between the values of the culture and our values as Christians. Training people to insist on their own rights will not make them more Christlike but only more self-interested. Scripture hardly mentions rights and then only the rights of the vulnerable ones.[9] Working for justice for all people (and sometimes ourselves) is vital work, but in the language of our faith, we are about welcome and hospitality and love (images that foster community) rather than rights (an image that fosters individualism and divisiveness).

Worship feels safe if *our* kind is named or pictured in the same ways that *their* kind is named and pictured. Worship feels welcoming if our world is reflected on the bulletin board, in the sermon illustrations, in the stories of the faith. Worship feels inclusive when there is reasonable accommodation to our limitations. Inclusive worship deepens our relationship with God and community, broadens our capacity for compassion, and puts us in the business of modeling the realm of God.

Practice #9

Integrate Music More Fully

The culture of music has gradually moved away
from a participative mode ... toward a performance
mode ... . (But) the church is a singing community;
(it) should be proud of being countercultural ... .
Congregational singing is an identity-shaping activity.
. —*John L. Bell*[1]

Those of us who are regular churchgoers may well open our
hymnbooks more often than we open our Bibles. It is likely that our
deepest and most powerful memories of church will involve music.
Many of us will define who we are by the music we sing. We need,
therefore, to look at the power of music to deepen worship. In this
chapter, I show how music can help us create worship that leads people deeper, worship that takes us out of our heads and into our hearts
and souls.

In all the churches I have served, I've been blessed with wonderful musicians who supported me and were creative in their own right.
From them I learned a lot and discovered how satisfying and produc-
tive it is to be part of a worship team. But that is not always the case.
Sometimes the relationship between clergy and musicians is heavy
with tension as both defend their turf and clutch to their vision. If the
pastor or worship leader is reading this chapter, remember that the
suggestions here are generally not things you do; they are things you

invite your musicians to do. Your musicians will have their own visions, experiences, and convictions. You will work best with them if you invite them into an understanding of why you do what you do, and of course, you will want to take advantage of their gifts, their creativity, their knowledge. No matter how committed you are to your vision of worship, you'll want to be open enough to receive from the musicians and humble enough to learn from them.

I am a strong advocate of not only music, but also other arts such as theater, dance, and the visual arts in worship. Like music, these mediums can bring the gospel to life, enable people to remember what they might otherwise forget, and most of all, open people to the deeper places of Spirit and their own souls. Once Debra brought her potter's wheel to worship when we planned a service around the biblical image of the potter and the clay (Jeremiah 18), and for another service, Frank brought some of his oil paintings and shared how his art was an expression of his faith. Here I am writing only about music because that is what is most commonly available to churches and because it is the creative art about which I know most. But I encourage you to find the various artistic talents in your congregation and invite them to join you in the effort to lead people more deeply into the gospel. In any case, music usually opens people's hearts more quickly than anything else in worship. How can we build on that capacity?

Congregational Singing

There is so much joy and power in congregational singing! How can we use that joy and power to nurture spiritual depth?

We are all familiar with the draining effect of hymns played too slowly. We recognize that music played too fast also alters the tone of worship, bringing people back to their heads and perhaps losing their participation. We know that some hymns are mournful, some are prayers, and some carry our marching orders; these should sound very different one from another. If your accompanist makes the lament sound like a lament, the congregation will find themselves going into places of compassion and understanding, into the deep places of their own lives that they may not usually visit. If prayer music is quiet and reflective, it will take people into the deep quiet of prayer. However, if all the music in the service is played at about the same tempo and volume, the people will stay pretty much in their thinking, surface selves.

Music can be part of the natural flow of the service, or it can disrupt that flow. It can invite us into our hearts, or keep us in our heads. Let's look again at an example we discussed previously. Imagine that you read the gospel, there is a pause of a few seconds, and the organist plays the musical response all the way through, finally holding one sustained chord. When the congregation begins singing, the connection between the gospel and the response will have been lost. What was to have been a joyful response to the Word has become just the next event in the worship order. Instead, after you read the gospel, if the organist immediately moves the people into the sung response by simply holding the first chord very briefly, the congregation will in fact be singing a response to the good news they just heard. The difference in this subtle change is remarkable. If you are concerned about establishing the tempo, the organist can play the last chord three times in tempo, followed by a one-beat rest; this sets the tempo, signals the congregation to begin singing, and still keeps the momentum going after the gospel reading.

Some congregations announce each hymn: "Now, let us stand and sing together number 262." If this is your community's habit, think about it. Why do you do this if people have a bulletin? If there is no significant reason for it, I encourage you to drop this practice. Each such announcement brings people back into their heads. For instance, suppose you just spoke a unison confession and then the worship leader offered the words of God's pardon. You could go immediately, without musical introduction, into singing "Amazing Grace" as your response to that pardon; you will either sing it by heart or you will ask the congregation to open their hymnals to page 547 before you began the prayer of confession. Moving so immediately into the hymn allows the music to be a reflection of the people's feelings at the moment; it is a vehicle giving an outlet to those feelings. On the other hand, look at an alternative scenario: After the pardon, the worship leader says, "Let's all stand and sing 'Amazing Grace,' which you'll find in your black hymnals on page 547." Worshipers reach for their hymnals and flip pages, the pianist plays the song through once, and the people finally begin to sing. In this scenario, the congregation is no longer singing a heartfelt response to God's forgiveness; that was lost when the spontaneity and immediacy of the response were lost. Now the congregation is just doing the next agenda item in the bulletin.

If you carefully choose a hymn or musical response and place it in a particular point of the service, then it is an important part of the flow, and it may be part of bringing people into a place of prayer, or centering them, or opening them to God's goodness; announcements bring them out of that inner place of quiet or centeredness or openness. When we break the flow and mood of the service to announce hymns, we help turn the congregation into an audience and take away their chance to be participants and the opportunity to carry any emotions generated by worship to a natural resolution.

Another way that congregational singing can help deepen our faith happens when we learn hymns from other cultures and chants in other languages. This challenges our temptation to parochialism and invites us into the sufferings and the hopes of people who are different than ourselves.

The worship wars go on, and churches struggle between contemporary and traditional music (and worship styles). I have served a traditional church that did not want contemporary hymns, and I experienced the same struggle with a progressive church that thought they could never sing traditional hymns. Both churches changed their minds and their music. If you introduce new things slowly, if you explain why changes are happening, if you work with your musicians and your worship committee, and most of all if you love the people, you can worship with a more expansive repertoire, even if your congregation chooses one style of music most of the time.

You can include different music in the same service, or you can choose traditional hymns most of the time and contemporary hymns on occasional Sundays, or vice versa. You can sing African-American spirituals and hymns written by the Wesley brothers. You can sing music arranged by Bach and praise songs from African Christians. You can use a pipe organ or a keyboard or a dulcimer or drums or all of the above to accompany the congregation's singing.

Ask the choir to sing a new hymn for a week or two before you invite the congregation to try it. The pianist could play it as the offertory for a couple weeks. You might invite everyone to practice new music just before worship begins. Or choose a new hymn and sing it, at least a couple verses of it, every Sunday for a month. When you introduce an unfamiliar hymn, select old favorites for the other hymns that day.

Connect the new music to something the congregation values. A justice-oriented hymn might be linked to the church's commitment to peace; a repetitive chant, to the church's commitment to prayer.

Be patient with people's resistance. Music touches deep places inside us, and the struggle over changes in music is about much more than music. It might be about power and control or about security and comfort zones. A change in music might threaten sacred memories of childhood or links to people loved but long since gone. A new kind of music might seem to undermine our image of God, and that is scary to people. To include new music in your worship, move slowly but firmly, gently, and always with love.

Chanting is an ancient musical form of prayer and has always been part of the Christian repertoire. However, many churches are not experienced with chanting in worship. It is an excellent way to deepen the worship experience and strengthen the sense of community. If your congregation is not used to chanting, it will be worth the effort to introduce it slowly. Chants, short simple songs that are repeated many times, are a part of the religious practices of most of the world's spiritual traditions. The words, often taken from scripture, are brief and easy to remember. Chants are often learned and sung without printed music. The Taizé community[2] has made chanting accessible to many churches, and their chants are a wonderful place to start. Remember, though, that true chanting is not the same as singing a hymn. Its meditative repetition is intended to draw people deeper into quiet, deeper into their hearts and souls, deeper into God. Of course, you may choose to sing a chant only two or three times, especially when you are first learning it. But it is the repetitions that allow the deepening, and that can be very powerful. Like silence, though, if your congregation is not prepared for it, they will only feel uncomfortable. Do your homework before you try chanting for three minutes.

Solos and Special Music

Most churches are blessed with music in addition to congregational singing. People with vocal or instrumental gifts offer their music as part of worship. If you are a congregation blessed with much talent, you have received a gift and with it a challenge. It is a gift to offer music to people; it is a ministry to offer musicians a place to share their music. But it can be a challenge for a musically inclined congregation to keep the gospel, and not the music, in the center. Churches begin with the awareness of and appreciation for the gifts they have received: a talented choir director, an exceptional organ, fine soloists. They decide to make good use of these gifts, and they do; worship is rich with musical offerings. But over time, the role of music may begin to shift. Musicians do not work with the pastor, and although their music is beautiful, it has no connection to the theme of the service or the gospel of the day. Musicians begin explaining; the congregation begins applauding; and worship feels more and more like an audience listening to a concert, not a congregation worshiping together. Some churches hire musicians from outside the church, and there is no connection between the musicians and the congregation, strengthening the concert model of audience and performer. I have seen visiting musicians enter the sanctuary just before their piece and leave just after: They clearly had no intention of being part of the worshiping congregation. When that happens, we have lost our clarity about the role of music in congregational worship.

There is another issue to consider, a small issue that has a big impact. At a concert, we watch the musicians come onto the stage, find their music, and warm up their instruments just before the concert begins. In worship, if we watch musicians walk forward, adjust their music stands, and open their music, we move again into our heads and into the role of audience, with the musicians—not the gospel—at the center. This happens sometimes when the choir must move into place before they sing. I encourage you to be sensitive to the flow of worship. Musicians should be ready to share their gifts with minimal activity beforehand. They might walk quietly forward at the appropriate times, or you might design the order of worship so the musicians can walk forward during the last verse of the preceding hymn or move into place as the children leave the sanctuary after children's time. Music and music stands can be in place before the service begins. It is also important to do the sound check and rehearsal well before the congregation begins arriving; nothing is more disruptive of worship than microphone or other technical issues during the service, and listening to a rehearsal before worship changes the way it is received during the service. My hope is that the musical offerings are integral to the flow of the service, supporting that flow instead of interrupting it.

I pay a lot of attention to the flow of worship, and this sometimes affects those who offer special music. By the time a service is crafted, it may be quite disruptive to suddenly insert something for which we had not planned. As they prepare worship, good worship leaders are conscious of which parts will probably be moving, where to allow the emotion to linger for a moment, how to honor yet contain the emotion that a solo may trigger. They know which parts of the service will be energetic and joyful and which parts will be reflective, restful, and quiet. They know how to lead us in a smooth transition between those moods.

One Christmas Eve, less than an hour before the service, someone came to me wanting very much to sing a solo that night. There was no way at that point to insert unexpected music without breaking the flow of the service. This was also a service in which I gave no instructions or explanations; this was a high holy day, and we did not discuss, we experienced. Adding something for which neither the congregation nor other musicians were prepared would throw people out of worship and into thinking mode again. ("What's happening?" "Let me check my bulletin." "This isn't listed." "Did I miss something?") And so I said no, honoring the integrity of the service. (There are times, of course, when the service is not so tightly crafted, and I receive unexpected offers for special music with delight.)

I encourage musicians not to talk before their solo. I have known occasional exceptions to this, such as when a soloist's introduction explaining why this song moves him became an important part of the worship offering. But usually verbal explanations distract. When a soloist explains what she is going to sing and tells us that she sang it last week at her nephew's baptism in Texas, and she isn't really a singer but she'll do her best, and ends by saying she hopes we'll like it—when that happens, the congregation becomes an audience listening to a performer and critiquing the performance. A solo in church is not a performance; it is an act of worship offered to God, one that invites the congregation also to offer acts of worship—their prayers and praise—as the solo brings forth. We are all worshiping together, offering our gifts and helping, we hope, our fellow worshipers to encounter the movement of the Spirit. If there is something significant to say about a solo, it could be said during the announcements or welcome at the beginning of worship so it does not break the flow of the service.

If you want music to be integral to the service, the worship leader must plan the services far in advance and communicate themes clearly to the musicians. I found this to be a balancing act. Planning weeks ahead stifled creativity for me, but not doing so made it impossible for musicians to find and learn appropriate music. Giving the musicians the scripture or sermon titles in advance was not helpful; they needed me to be much more specific about the theme or focus for each week if I wanted the music to tie closely to the service. If the worship leader and musicians work toward being a team, sharing ownership for worship, you can find a way to accommodate the needs and creative styles of all.

More Ways to Integrate Music Fully in Worship

Let's look at some other ways to integrate music fully into the service and into the goal of deepening worship.

Music is such a powerful invitation to open our hearts. Quiet music behind the words of a prayer or certain scripture readings can bring worshipers into the prayer or scripture. Note, however, that if the music is a familiar hymn, the listener may focus on the tune or the memorized words and miss the scripture or prayer. It might be better for the organist to play something unfamiliar or to use soft chord progressions instead of a melody.

Change in worship practices often becomes an issue. Our world is so full of change and threats; people may value the security of sameness. Consider having one piece of music (such as a response after the prayer, offering, or benediction) that rarely changes. Don't eliminate the congregation's favorite hymn even if you do find the theology questionable.

On the other hand, change that is handled appropriately invigorates. Learn new hymns. Play music behind a spoken prayer some weeks, but not others. If you have the option, use different instruments in different ways in the service. Don't be afraid to sing a variety of hymns: traditional, contemporary, praise music, hymns from other cultures. Change the worship order as needed to accommodate the flow, the different moods, the shifting energies of worship.

We are used to thinking of special music as supporting a worship service: anthem or solo, prayer response, choral call to worship. We can expand our use of music by building an entire service around a musical selection, if we have the freedom to be creative in that way. (And if our church's tradition does not lend itself to this style of worship, we can easily adapt these ideas for a program after a potluck or the church's annual meeting.) For instance, "Moses" by Ken Medema[3] is a powerful piece, longer than a traditional anthem. In dramatic music, it tells the story of God's call to Moses. One Sunday in a church I served, that piece became both the scripture (Exodus 3) and sermon; the service was built around the theme of God's call to us. Another Sunday, we dedicated a child and used the music "I Hope You Dance" by Sanders, Sillers, and Womack.[4] The song is a wish that the child live life with great joy and courage and vitality, so I used that theme throughout the service. My sermon was about how we might raise children so they can indeed live that way. One week the men's quartet sang the Iona song "Sing Hey for the Carpenter,"[5] and I built worship around our response to Jesus' call to follow him into a life of prayer and service.

Another way to make good use of music is through the creative use of the hymns. Many churches are familiar with hymn sing Sundays; people either love them or hate them! You can take advantage of the ability of hymns not only to inspire but also to educate, and build a hymn sing around a theme. I have told the history of the Christian church through the careful selections of hymns. Once we shaped the service around the history of Christian music. We chose hymns representing different eras and styles of music, shared some very brief information about the hopes and struggles of the church in that time, sang a verse or two of a hymn from that period, and then moved on to the next musical era in the church's long, rich tradition.

This was interspersed with the normal elements of worship: prayer, children's time, offering, and so on. When we had no hymns to represent a historical period or musical style, we invited our musicians to share solos or anthems from that era. Another time I built a hymn sing service around the Apostles' Creed, and once around the Book of Psalms. We used words from the creed or psalms in various ways in the liturgies. Though there was no formal sermon, I talked briefly about one section of the creed or one kind of psalm. Then we sang a verse or two of a hymn that represented the same theme or theology as those lines of the creed or found a hymn that was a musical version of the psalm. Then we'd move on to the next section of the creed, or another psalm, continuing to intersperse some reading, some spoken words, and related music.

Although it wasn't a hymn sing Sunday, once we made good use of music by building a service around Bach. We sang and listened to his music, heard a brief sketch about his life and faith, and used that to look at how we use our gifts to glorify God. Another time we shaped worship around contemporary Christian music. In that case, I could have chosen to talk about one theme that appears in the music or about the way worship expressions change throughout history, or I might have used the music to lift up the biblical themes of praise and lament.

From my own painful experience, I offer you a warning: Don't make the service too crowded! That will be a temptation if you are building it around a theme such as Christian history or exploring the psalms. There is so much to say and so much music available to help you say it! But too much content will lose the congregation. Remember, less is more.

There are some concerns to address if you choose to plan worship in these less traditional ways. You need to be clear about what worship is and what its purpose is. It is easy to begin with the best intentions and unwittingly create a service in which the main purpose turns out to be entertainment or showcasing musicians. Remember to ask yourself the following questions as checks and balances: What is the good news that the chosen scripture proclaims? How does the planned service proclaim that same good news? Does the wisdom of scripture hold a central place in the service, or is it just tacked on because there is supposed to be a scripture reading? Have you talked with the musicians about the purpose of this worship and their role in it? Have you thought about, and talked with the musicians about, the difference between audience and congregation, between performers and worship leaders? Have all the people involved in the service prayed together about this worship?

Applause in Worship

Another issue that churches may struggle with is how the congregation should respond after a singer, instrumentalist, or group shares special music. Communities differ in their use of applause in worship. Some find it a natural way to show their gratitude, while others feel it is not appropriate in worship. Because of my hope that worship is planned in such a way as to take us deeper, I prefer not to have applause during worship. I have experienced occasional exceptions to this. I join eagerly in applause during our time of sharing and announcements when we congratulate Norman and Chris who celebrate their sixtieth wedding anniversary. But during the worship liturgy, applause usually tends to confirm that we are an audience listening to a performer and that it is appropriate for us to critique that performer in the midst of worship. If the solo moves us deeply, then the most appropriate response is a moment or two of silence and stillness after the music ends. Imagine the following possibilities during worship:

Jane has been through two years of a life-threatening illness. We have been praying for her in church every week. We wonder how she had the courage to keep struggling when her situation often seemed hopeless. At last, she seems to be recovering, and after being back to church for only a couple weeks, she sings a powerful solo about God's presence in time of trouble. It is a good song, and she has a good voice, but those are not what are important. Jane's singing is so powerful for us because we know what she has been through; we know her own struggles about whether God was present or not. We are moved by her life and her musical witness. There are tears on many cheeks.

Reverend Alex stands up as soon as she finishes and cheerfully says, "Thank you, Jane. That was beautiful. We really appreciate your music. Let's all show Jane how grateful we are." And he leads us in a round of applause. What does that feel like?

Or it might happen this way: When Jane finishes, the sanctuary is absolutely silent—what I call a pin-drop moment. There is no coughing, no shuffling, no looking in the bulletin for what comes next—just silence. Reverend Alex remains in his seat for several seconds after the music ends, giving us the gift of allowing us to be where we are and feel what we are feeling. When he does get up, he does so slowly. He takes a step or two quietly, not speaking; his unobtrusive movements are a gentle warning that in just a moment, we will move from that deep place. He may nod at Jane, or mouth a silent "thank you." Still in silence, he picks up his Bible and opens to the text, giving us more time to return from the deep place to which Jane's witness took us. Finally he looks at us, and without any abrasive change in mood, he says, "Our gospel reading this morning is from ..." The congregation sighs; the moment is past. We were allowed to experience the moment; we were allowed to be in the place the music took us; and then Reverend Alex gently and respectfully brought us back to the present. Do you think this silence and this honoring of the silence communicated to Jane as much as the applause did? Or more?

I can imagine one other scenario. This one includes applause, but the feeling is quite different. Jane finishes singing. The tears are there; the total silence is there. No one moves for a moment, and Reverend Alex allows us to remain in the silence. Then, in a spontaneous tribute to Jane's struggle, to her courage and her witness, one congregant stands up, and then another, and another; and someone begins applauding, and in the middle of worship, Jane receives a standing ovation. But it happened in such a way that everyone knows it is not about thanking her for her music (though we do) but about thanking her for the courage she has modeled for us and thanking God for the gift that she is and for her return to us. Can you see what a different role the applause plays here than in the first scenario?

This third scenario is the exception. Applause does not usually deepen worship. But it is true that sometimes we are so moved by music—and someone's gift of music—and so filled, that it is hard not to respond. It is like the emotion of it caused us to hold our breath and we need to let it out. There is an old tradition in the church for people to murmur "Amen" or "Alleluia" or "Thanks be to God." I like these responses. Because people do not do that at concert halls or theaters, it reminds us that we are not an audience; we are a congregation. We are not consumers; we are church. Such a response uses our own language, reminding us that our worship is centered on God, not on any one performer, and not on our own emotions.

Music is so powerful! I encourage you to work closely with your musicians, to use their gifts and their insights, and to fully integrate music so that it proclaims the gospel and takes people more deeply into the love of God.

Practice #10

Insist on Integrity in the Worship Service

(A) Christianity lived only ego-deep
will ultimately betray itself.
—*Cynthia Bourgeault*[1]

When considering the integrity of the worship service, I am not referring to the integrity of the pastor or worship leader, although I certainly hope that is present. I am referring to integrity in the service itself. If a worship service is to have integrity, concern for that begins in the planning process. No, it begins *before* the planning process: It begins with the prayer life of the pastor, as we saw in Practice #1. Reading scripture in a way that bores people tarnishes the integrity of worship (see Practice #4). Designing worship so that all parts support the theme of the day's scripture is an issue of integrity in worship (see Practice #5). How worship includes or excludes certain people: isn't that about integrity (see Practice #8)? And Practice #9 lifts up integrity issues that relate to music. You see, we've been talking about worship integrity in every chapter of this book. In this final chapter, I will raise a few remaining issues that honor or mar the integrity of worship.

Integrity is *the quality of possessing and steadfastly adhering to high moral principles or professional standards.* Something that has integrity is true to its deepest self. It is authentic. It is what it says it is. It does what it says it will do. Its appearances and its reality are congruent. It is integral to the whole. With that in mind, let's walk through a typical service to see what issues come up with regards to integrity.

Call to Worship

Some churches prefer the traditional language of worship, such as *prelude* and *call to confession*. Other congregations use contemporary language, such as *gathering music* and *telling the truth about our lives*. The issue of integrity here is not about what we call it, but whether or not we do what we're saying. The call to worship should do what it says: call us together for the specific purpose of worship and prepare us to come before God. It is more than just the sign that the service is beginning. If the call to worship is used as a place to plug in a nice reading or special music that has nothing to do with calling the people of God to the act of worship, then the integrity is marred. Similarly, does the invocation actually invoke? *Invocation* is not just a word meaning *prayer at the beginning of worship*. An invocation has a very specific purpose: *To invoke* means *to call forth* or *to summon*, so an invocation is a prayer that asks God to be present in our worship, or asks the Christ energy to come, or asks Spirit to move among us. Such a prayer can be spoken by the worship leader or printed in the bulletin, but sometimes I help congregations to understand the significance of invocation by opening worship with an invitation to "call in the spirits." I might begin like this: "Today in worship, we are talking about Jesus' command to love our enemies. We are not alone in the difficult struggle to obey this command. We are surrounded by spirits and energies that are eager to help us. Let's invite them to be present now; let's call them to our aid. What quality or virtue helps you love when it is hard to do so? Or perhaps there is a saint in the church whose life or teaching empowers you to Christlike love. Maybe the most loving saint you know was your grandfather. Let's invite this great cloud of witnesses, these good energies, to be present in our worship. I call Jesus to come into our midst today." After my words, congregants call for the spirits they wish to invoke, the energies that can help them love their enemies. Someone might call out, "the spirit of courage"; another might name Martin Luther King Jr. Others might ask for the spirits of forgiveness and peace or the spirit of Julian of Norwich. This is a true invocation. Like a good call to worship, it prepares us. It invites us out of our familiar place of busyness and analysis and control and into a space of openness and humility and hope. A call to worship or invocation has integrity when it makes it clear that we are suspending business as usual and are coming to stand in the presence of Ultimate Reality.

Confession and Pardon

If you have a prayer of confession in your worship, is it really a confession, or is it something else? I have seen many prayers labeled *confession* that praised God's goodness but never really baldly and humbly confessed our sins.

The Assurance of Pardon is not an encouragement to do better next time. It is not a reassurance that we're lovable after all. It is not the pastor telling us about God's mercy. The pardon, though using the pastor as a conduit, is an act of God.

Do the confessions and pardons in your worship allow the power of God to reach the people?

Children's Time

There are similar integrity issues for the children's time. We discussed some of these concerns in Practice #8, so here is just a quick reminder: Is children's time really for children, or is it for the entertainment of the adults? If children's time is for the children, the leader will sit down with the children to be at their level instead of towering over them. The conversation will be about concrete situations, not abstract theologies. The leader will use words a small child can under-stand and avoid the multisyllable words or jargon that adults take for granted. The message will be conveyed in ways that speak to children: through story or experience (an activity) instead of through concepts and abstractions. The children will explore the same theme or scrip-ture that the rest of the service offers. When we insist on the integri-ty of the worship service, children's time is truly for the children.

Scripture and Sermon

Many issues of integrity surround scripture and preaching: Is the preaching authentic? Is the pastor preaching from lived experience (his own or that of the Body) or offering platitudes that do not hon-estly reflect the pastor's or people's lives? Is the preaching a vehicle to make the gospel more accessible to the people, or is it a chance to showcase the preacher's life and skills? Does the preacher hold togeth-er the scripture and people's real lives in this time and place? If we only preach about what happened two thousand years ago, we violate the integrity of scripture, which carries not just history but universal and eternal truths. If we only preach about today's issues, with scrip-ture an expendable veneer on the surface, we violate the integrity of scripture which offers us ground on which to stand in the midst of today's issues.

Is the preacher clear about the difference between the worldview of the gospel and the worldview of the culture, and clear about which is being offered in worship? The worship leader needs a good under-standing of different models of reality. If we are not very clear what story we are living out of, we will, without realizing it, live out of the culture's story, because it is so subtle and so persuasive and so promi-nent. But we committed ourselves at baptism (or confirmation) to liv-ing out of God's story, which is not the same as the culture's story. For instance, Walter Wink explores the culture's story of redemptive vio-lence ("Violence will save you.") versus Jesus' story of redemptive love

("Only love will save you.").[2] As worship leaders, it is essential that we immerse ourselves in scripture and the great saints and holy people of the faith (and of other faiths), so that the gospel model gets into our cells and bones. Unless we are clear that we are offering the gospel's view of reality, there is no integrity in our worship.

Another issue of integrity is whether our worship is honest, naming what is. Some churches seem to communicate that worshipers are to check their pain at the door. Sometimes we unwittingly encourage people to live out of a persona, hiding their deepest struggles and sins. Perhaps, in the desire not to be unpleasant, we never talk about sexual abuse in church. We avoid using controversial words such as *lesbian* or *bisexual*. Our stories, curriculum, and sermon illustrations assume that every family is made up of mom, dad, and two kids even though that is no longer the norm even in our own congregation. We celebrate the joy of Christmas without acknowledging what a painful time it can be. On the other hand, in some churches it is the joy that we're not to bring to worship. We are so focused on the pain of Christmas that we don't allow the joy to be present. We are so concerned about war and oppression that we fail to delight in life and bring laughter into our worship. Our lives are messier than we like to admit and more wondrous than we usually acknowledge. They require both lamentation and celebration. The preacher must hold together both suffering and hope. If our preaching is to have integrity, it must tell the truth about our lives.

Sometimes the issue of integrity comes up when we invite a guest preacher to worship. Does that person feed the people, offering them the gospel? Or does she really use that time to inform people about her program, cause, or agency? It is certainly appropriate to educate people about the mission of the children's home that their denomination supports, but unless that information becomes a tool that helps us worship, perhaps it belongs in another context. It is about integrity.

Prayer

Issues of integrity come up in prayer too. Are the prayers really directed toward God, or are they directed toward the people? Do they turn into mini sermons? This is a very common issue in churches and one of the most blatant violations of integrity. Of course, we can say that God does not need our words at all; the best prayer directed to God would be silence. I hope there is some silence in your worship. But we use words because it is an authentic mode of communication for us, and because as worship leaders, we speak on behalf of the people, and so they have a right to hear what we are saying. The words need to honestly reflect what the people (including the pastor) want to say to God, not what the pastor wants the people to hear.

If your congregation offers people an opportunity to pray aloud or offer joys and concerns that will be integrated into a prayer, notice whether the prayers really reflect your lives. It seems much easier for us to name our concerns than our joys, as if pain and fear are the only truths in our world. Whatever struggles we face, our lives are also rich with blessings. Our prayers should hold both. It's about integrity.

Offering

How is the offering received in your church? Does it feel like an intermission? Does it seem like a break in the service, with little connection to the rest of worship? It, too, needs to have integrity.

In one church I attended, the ushers received the offering, and when they retrieved the baskets from the last row, they left the sanctuary to count the money. The gifts were never brought forward to the altar or table to symbolize that they were being offered to God. No prayer or ritual dedicated them to that purpose; there was no opportunity for communal ownership of the gifts. And this practice removed the ushers from the rest of worship, as if to say it wasn't that important anyway. These are issues of integrity.

In one church where I served as pastor, the offering ritual never changed, and the prayers became quite mechanical. In another church I served, there were no prayers or ritual around the offering, and it seemed disconnected from worship. I now think that in both of these churches, I failed to handle this part of worship with integrity.

How is the offering an act of worship? That question can lead us back to integrity. Can you remember a time when you felt the offering in church was significant and worshipful? Can you identify what made it feel that way?

An offering has integrity when it is an integral part of worship. That might happen when we place it in the order of worship in such a way that it becomes a response to God's grace or an opportunity for discipleship. The offering is integral to the service when we use that time for worship. In many churches, the offering feels like an intermission. The energy relaxes, and people shuffle in their seats and whisper to their neighbor. It becomes a good time to look at the bulletin to see what comes next.

What if the offering engaged the congregation as much as the anthem or the prayers? Worshipers might be invited into silent prayers of thanksgiving; the pastor could help by suggesting some minimal structure to keep the congregation focused, saying something such as "Spend this time thanking God for every blessing you can think of, one blessing at a time." Or the pastor might invite them to offer specific prayers as they put their offering in the plate, prayers for a particular mission or ministry that the offering supports, or prayers for a person in need. The pastor could invite them to hold the plate for a few seconds as they pray; slowing the offering helps integrate it into worship, and if time is a concern, compensate by using more ushers. Sometimes people can come forward to bring their offering to the altar. Perhaps their offering can include canned goods for the food pantry or blankets for refugees. The pastor can use sermons or litanies to remind us that giving our money is just a symbol of what we really offer: our whole selves for God's use. Many churches sing the

Doxology as they dedicate the offering: a hymn of praise for the gifts we've received and that we share. Chanting during the offering is another option: The Taizé chants *"Ubi caritas Deus ibi est"* ("Where there is selfless love, God is truly there")[3] or *"Laudate Dominum"* ("Sing, praise, and bless the Lord")[4] would work well. The point is not to fill the time with something, but to engage the congregation so that they are mindful of *offering.*

Words of invitation or dedication can connect the offering to the main theme of the worship or the day's gospel. If the service is about peace, the offering might be a symbol of the community's renewed commitment to work for peace in specific ways. If the gospel reading is about prayer, perhaps the offering reminds the people what prayer is—offering our energies for God's use. When the offering has been received, someone must bring it forward so the congregation can recognize this communal gift and dedicate it—and themselves.

One obvious thing to consider when we discuss offering integrity is the stewardship practiced by you, the pastor or church leader. Do you tithe? Can you speak from personal experience about the joys and freedom that come with tithing? If not, you cannot preach with integrity about tithing. How does your spending reflect, or fail to reflect, the values that you preach? How attached are you to possessions, to comfort, to status? Unless you wrestle with such issues, you cannot—with integrity—invite your congregation to do so.

Education about stewardship is an ongoing task. The offering gives us a weekly opportunity to do that. Can we help people to recognize their checkbooks and appointment calendars as spiritual documents? These tell us what we really value.

Worship can help us make connections between our faith and our possessions, between our discipleship and our impact on the planet. Worship can remind us that the spiritual life is about letting go, not only of our material goods, but of our fears and prejudices and efforts at control. Letting go is a kind of offering. The offering symbolizes surrender and relinquishment, both virtues of our faith. The offering gives us a way to talk about the culture's model of consumerism and the gospel's model of community. Just as we choose to give our money to mission and ministry instead of buying some new delight, we are reminded that such a value makes us aliens in the culture. When these reflections are integral to the life of the church, then the offering has integrity.

Communion

When we celebrate the Eucharist, when we offer communion to our people, we meet more issues of integrity. Our traditions debate the nature and interpretation of communion, and we differ on other details as well: Are children welcome? May the elements be blessed and served by anyone or only ordained clergy? Who may come to the table? Do we use wine or juice, wafers or broken bread? These are significant issues, but here we will only take on more practical issues. How we serve communion can also raise issues of integrity.

We have named the Eucharist as a sacrament, one of our most sacred acts, one that brings the grace of God to us. And yet, in many churches, it is done with so little feeling and so much haste that many people admit to finding little meaning in it. Worship leaders, especially the pastor or priest, do well to check in with themselves now and then. Is communion meaningful for you? Do you speak the words with intention because they are so life-giving for you, or have they become rote and mechanical? Do you feel that you offer a tremendous gift to Tony and Linda and Kay, people whom you love? Your answer to these questions will put you in touch with your own relationship with the sacrament at this moment in your ministry. The sacrament will be a vehicle for God's grace regardless of the state of the pastor, but when your heart is open to receive God's gift, it will be easier for your people to come with open hearts too.

I hope you plan worship so that communion is unhurried, so that you do not squeeze it into an already full service with one eye on the clock. If you have the freedom to use different communion liturgies, do you ever do so? Find the balance between fresh expressions that can stir new insights and ancient words that stand the test of time. Look at the arrangement of your sanctuary. Is the communion table near the people so they are pulled into your words and actions? Or is it far removed from them, as if what is happening does not concern them? Remember to make eye contact with the people as you speak the words and break the bread.

I believe that there is so much sacred energy around communion, it is almost too hot to handle. And yet, sometimes the way we serve communion in our churches feels like we wrapped it in asbestos to make sure the energy won't come through. If you are willing to ponder some of these reflections, you may find that new life begins to emerge from this sacrament.

When I serve communion, I want there to be integrity in my words and actions. If I speak about the power of this sacrament to transform us, I look for any experience of transformation happening in worship. If I mention awe and mystery, I try to offer the sacrament in such a way as to convey an experience of awe and mystery. Because I name the breaking of the bread, I don't slice the bread ahead of time. Actions are even more powerful than words; if I want to convey that Jesus' body was broken, I want the bread to rip and tear (I do check the bread beforehand, and if it has a hard crust, I make a cut of about an inch in the bottom so that I can in fact break it without a knife). When I talk about Jesus' blood poured out for many, I pour the wine so we can see and hear that pouring out. This engages our whole bodies, awakens our senses, touches more than just our minds.

People are more likely to be drawn into the sacrament if they are participants in the liturgy. Of course, they can speak words printed in the bulletin, but they can also echo the words of institution, one phrase at a time—and this is more powerful if it is not in print. You can invite the people to raise their hands in the gesture of blessing to bless the elements. When I invite various congregations to such simple ways of sharing the liturgy, people always tell me afterward how important communion was for them that day.

I rarely hear worship leaders invite people to slow down so they can really absorb the sacrament, and to be present in the sacred moment. Especially when people leave their pews and come forward to receive communion, the line may move quickly, and congregants have no more than a couple seconds to take the elements and then hurry out of the way. There is not much of a chance for opening or deepening here! A few words about this can call people back to the present moment and remind them to slow down, to savor this feast, to take this sacrament seriously, to allow themselves to be fed, to absorb the nurturing of this act. What about the lining up itself or the waiting in the pews? What is that like in your church? Is it a time for prayer or singing? Is there an air of expectation or inner preparation? Is it an opportunity for mindfulness? Or is it akin to waiting in line at McDonald's, where the waiting has no significance of its own? Perhaps you can discourage the chatter or restlessness that might go on at this time, and invite people to be aware that the waiting is part of the sacrament. God's goodness comes to us, but it comes in the midst of waiting and sharing.

Holy Communion is a profoundly nurturing act. Our sacrament of communion has overtones of lovemaking (taking my Beloved's body into my own) and of breast-feeding ("Our beloved mother Jesus," as fourteenth-century English anchoress Julian of Norwich says, "feeds us with himself"[5]). It brings up the emotions of being a guest at the table of a generous and loving host who is providing us not just with food, but also with beauty, rest, comfort, shelter, and renewal: profound hospitality. We are a people who, most of us, are always meeting obligations and caring for others; here we are at last the receivers: Someone is caring for us. This sacrament of ours touches deep primordial feelings, many of them unconscious but still operative. It is so important that we invite people to this table and offer them this feast in ways that honor (and free) those deepest feelings and associations, though people may never name them in words.

I notice the peoples' response when they receive communion from a server (this can also apply to communion served in the pews when people pass the elements to one another). Some people take the bread and cup without ever looking at the server. I regret that when I serve communion because I value the eye contact. The eyes are the windows of the soul. Allowing someone to look us in the eye is allowing ourselves to be vulnerable. It invites connection. It offers honesty and openness. Looking another person in the eye moves us from our thinking selves to a place of communion. When I serve communion, I look each person in the eye and, when possible, address each by name: "Angie, this is the Body of Christ, broken for you," "Steve, the cup of blessing." I have received much feedback from parishioners about this; they can experience communion as a gift because it is offered to them in such a loving, personal way.

Occasionally, someone will use the moment I serve communion to them to compliment me: "Your sermon meant so much to me," or "This is a fine service." I find that very distressing! This is not a time to focus on me for any reason. I also notice that many people thank the server. I understand the intent, of course, but when I receive a "thank you" for offering communion, it is disconcerting. Do they think this is *my* food being offered? Do they think *I* am the source of this gift? I like to be thanked for many things, but not for communion. Even though I am in the role of server at that moment, we are both of us just hungry people coming to the place where there is bread.

It is possible to talk to people about communion, about slowing down and being in the moment. You can preach about this or integrate words and practices into worship. You can help people think about what communion means and what it means for each of them. You can help them honor the mystery, even when they do not understand. If you suggest words for both the servers and the communicants to say, they will have tools that will put them at ease and help them reclaim this ancient sacrament. Servers might say "The Body of

Christ, broken for you" or "The bread of life" or "The cup of blessing" or whatever words your tradition uses. You might invite those receiving the elements to respond with a phrase such as "Thanks be to God" or "Amen" or "Blessed be." Perhaps this will help to remove the emphasis from the server and place the emphasis on the gift and the Giver.

Benediction

Let's look at one final issue of integrity: Is the benediction a blessing, which is what the word *benediction* means? Or is it really a *charge*? A *charge* is important and appropriate, reminding people of the commission to take the good news of love and justice to all people, but don't call that a benediction! A charge tells people to do something: "Go forth into this week, and bring the good news of God's love to all you meet," or "Feed the hungry. Comfort the grieving. Welcome the stranger." These are charges. A benediction, however, is not about what we are to do; it is entirely about what God does. And it is not *telling* us about God's action; it *is* God's action. A benediction is a gift given to us from God, given freely without our having to earn it, with no concern about our worthiness. It is grace poured out upon us. It is simply for us to receive.

I find that many churches print the word *benediction* in the bulletin, but the words spoken at that point in the service are really a charge. When I am a worshiper, I want that benediction. I know that I can't live out the charge unless I have received the blessing that will empower me. When the benediction is not a benediction at all, but a charge, I feel cheated. I leave hungry. In fact, I often feel angry. It is the pastor's job to serve as the channel for God's grace to pour upon me so I can live out the demands of discipleship. I need to receive that grace. I need it.

Sometimes I wonder if the reason many churches offer charges instead of benedictions (or a long charge and a quick benediction of

sorts tacked on as an afterthought) is because many of us, especially
in the more liberal expressions of the church, are no longer sure that
there is any God to pour grace upon us. We are comfortable with
charges: They depend on human effort, and that is what we trust. We
are comfortable with charges: They tell us to get busy and work harder, and we know how to do both those things very well. We are comfortable with charges. But a benediction implies that there is a Source
beyond ourselves for grace: We don't have to do it ourselves; it is not
all up to us. That belief flies in the face of our culture's convictions,
which many churches have unfortunately adopted for their own. I
name as anemic those benedictions that seem to imply "I'm sorry
there isn't really a God capable of pouring grace on you, but I want to
offer you my best wishes." This is the "have-a-good-day" kind of blessing, and it violates the integrity of worship.

When I offer a benediction, I believe that it is not coming from
me. I am not blessing the people; God is. I am just offering myself as
the channel. I always use the ancient sign of blessing, the outstretched
arm or upraised hand and the sign of the cross, because I believe that
energy literally passes from Ultimate Reality through me to the people. Because God is intent on blessing the people, if I do not allow that
to happen, I am stealing a gift that was given to them. I believe that
being the channel through which God blesses the people is one of my
most central pastoral functions. It is not that only pastors can offer
benedictions; it is just that ordination sets pastors apart to make that
one of our primary life tasks: to bless the people and to offer ourselves
as a channel through which God blesses the people.

I have received many comments about the benedictions in the
worship services I lead, because people feel the blessing they are
receiving and it feeds them. When I offer a benediction, I am usually
able to move into that part of the service with intention, maybe taking a deep breath or standing for a moment or two in silence before I
begin. This allows me to focus on the gift I am about to pass on to
them, and it allows the people to open themselves in expectation. I

speak the benediction from my heart; I do not read it. There are powerful benedictions in print, and I may borrow from one or memorize part of one, but when I offer the final blessing to the people, I do not read it. I speak deliberately and make eye contact with many people: After all, these words are sacred gifts for them; I want them to know they are receiving a gift. Often I include some blessing that relates to the theme we shared through worship, the good news of the scripture we read that day: "Remember, God has written your name on the palm of God's hand. Go into this week knowing that nothing you can do can take away God's love for you. You are precious in God's sight. Go in peace." Because I love words and respect their beauty and power, I sometimes speak benedictions that are somewhat poetic. But I also add words that are simple and direct, usually about God's love for the people. And if I offer a charge, it always comes first, because it is important to me that the last thing congregants experience in worship is God blessing them.

Concluding Thoughts

I hope that these thoughts about integrity in worship will encourage you to look at your services, reconsidering weak areas and strengthening those parts that you already do well. We teach integrity by modeling it in everything we do, even in the planning and leading of worship. Considering the integrity of worship is also about deepening worship. Issues of integrity challenge us to look more deeply at what we do in worship, and that is very likely to cause us to do things that inevitably deepen our worship. We deepen our worship when we invite people out of their heads, out of their in-control, evaluating, thinking selves, and when, at least for moments, they are free to move into their hearts and souls where they encounter their true selves—and God. This is where they lower their defenses (which come from our heads, our ego selves) and feel safe enough to be open; that openness makes it possible to receive God's love or to perceive God's movement in their lives. When worship has integrity, people access energy and healing and hope. For the well-being of your people and yourself, insist on the integrity of the worship service, and know that in that effort, God will bless you.

Benediction

**For the kingdom of God depends
not on talk but on power.**
—1 Corinthians 4:20 (NRSV)

While I worked on this book, I worshiped in about twenty-five different churches in several denominations and in various parts of the country. In previous years, I worshiped in many more. In some of those churches, I was greatly blessed, but too often, I came hungry and went home hungry. Sometimes I cried through those services: cried for my yearnings, cried for my hopes, cried for what could be but wasn't. More often, I got angry.

What triggered that anger was sometimes visible: The people looked bored. The energy was flat. We heard about new life and we sang about new life, but we didn't experience new life. Sometimes, the cause of my anger was less visible: The service was very head-centered; it never opened hearts or souls. It was based on consumer models or therapy models. *Knowing about* God was assumed to be the same as *knowing* God. God's power was reduced to the best the human mind could comprehend. I thought of Jesus overturning the tables in the temple because the leaders used the deep tools of Spirit for purposes other than connecting the people to Spirit.

While visiting these churches, I did not find that there is one right way to worship. Quaker silence or Catholic high church or African drums: Christian tradition embraces a huge variety of worship expressions, and each can open our hearts, deepen our faith, and lead us to our Source and Spirit. Each holds a part of the treasure that we call the Christian faith. And yet in many of our churches, there is today a profound crisis of Spirit. We are sitting on a whale, fishing for minnows.

Sometimes as I sit in the pew struggling with the anger that rises up in me, I want to shout at the clergy: "These people are so hungry! You have no right to be their pastor and not feed them!" But how can the clergy feed the people if the clergy themselves are starving?

I hope this book helps you to learn some ways to deepen your worship so that hungry people will find food. But if you apply what you learn here as if it were a collection of tricks and techniques, not much will change. Deepening your church's worship demands that you live and lead out of a place of deep prayer. How can you show people God's love if you have not tasted it yourself? How can you preach peace if your own inner life is in constant turmoil? How can you be a non-anxious presence in the face of a parishioner's faith crisis if you have not wrestled with searing doubts yourself? If your sources of healing are no different than those your parishioners see on TV talk shows, how can you offer them life? How can you feed your people if you do not yourself know where to find bread?

We are all wounded healers,[1] full of our own struggles and inadequacies. The grace is that we don't need to have it all together to do this work, thank goodness. Spirit moving among us will make up for our deficiencies. We and our people can grow and deepen together. The transforming agent is not our worship but grace. Relax, make changes slowly, and trust that any little bit helps. Most of all, work on yourself more than on your worship.

Sometimes worship needs a major overhaul, but little changes are often enough to make a difference. Many of the suggestions in this book can be integrated into your Sunday services without profound changes in the outward appearance of worship. And yet there will be profound changes. If you plan and lead worship in ways that make it safe for people to go into the depths of their souls and of our tradition, you will indeed see profound changes—in the health and vibrancy of your community, in the lives of the people, and in yourself, the worship leader. It will be as if Spirit is unburied and set free in your midst. It will be Grace, coming to dwell among you.

Further Reading

Bass, Diana Butler. *Christianity for the Rest of Us: How the Neighborhood Church is Transforming the Faith.* New York: HarperOne, 2006.

Begbie, Jeremy S. *Resounding Truth: Christian Wisdom in the World of Music.* Grand Rapids: Baker Academic, 2007.

Berglund, Brad. *Reinventing Sunday: Breakthrough Ideas for Transforming Worship.* Valley Forge, PA: Judson Press, 2001.

Bourgeault, Cynthia. *Chanting the Psalms.* Boston: New Seeds Books, 2006.

———. *Centering Prayer and Inner Awakening.* Cambridge: Cowley Publications, 2004.

Bruteau, Beatrice. *Radical Optimism: Practical Spirituality in an Uncertain World.* Boulder: Sentient Publications, 2002.

Co, Stephen, and Eric B. Robins, MD, with John Merryman. *Your Hands Can Heal You.* New York: Free Press, division of Simon & Schuster, Inc., 2002.

Dawn, Marva J. *Reaching Out without Dumbing Down: A Theology of Worship for the Turn-of-the-Century Culture.* Grand Rapids: Wm. B. Eerdmans, 1995.

———. *A Royal "Waste" of Time: The Splendor of Worshiping God and Being Church for the World.* Grand Rapids: Wm. B. Eerdmans, 1999.

Doughty, Steve. *To Walk in Integrity: Spiritual Leadership in Times of Crisis.* Nashville: Upper Room Books, 2004.

Easwaran, Eknath. *God Makes the Rivers to Flow: Selections from the Sacred Literature of the World.* Tomales, CA: Nilgiri Press, 1991.

Hauerwas, Stanley, and William H. Willimon. *Resident Aliens: A Provocative Christian Assessment of Culture and Ministry for People Who Know that Something is Wrong.* Nashville: Abingdon Press, 1989.

Keating, Thomas. *Intimacy with God: An Introduction to Centering Prayer.* New York: The Crossroad Publishing Co., 1994.

Law, Eric H.F. *The Wolf Shall Dwell with the Lamb: A Spirituality for Leadership in a Multicultural Community.* St. Louis: Chalice Press, 1993.

Leal, Douglas. *Stop Reading and Start Proclaiming!* San Jose: Resource Publications, 2006.

Long, Thomas G. *Beyond the Worship Wars: Building Vital and Faithful Worship.* Herndon, VA: The Alban Institute, 2001.

Lozoff, Bo. *It's a Meaningful Life: It Just Takes Practice.* New York: Penguin Group (USA) Inc., 2000.

Marion, Jim. *Putting on the Mind of Christ: The Inner Work of Christian Spirituality.* Charlottesville, VA: Hampton Roads Publishing Company, Inc., 2000.

Merrill, Nan C. *Psalms for Praying: An Invitation to Wholeness.* New York: The Continuum International Publishing Group Inc., 2003.

Ministry & Liturgy. San Jose: Resource Publications, Inc., www.ministryandliturgy.com.

Peterson, Eugene H. *The Contemplative Pastor: Returning to the Art of Spiritual Direction*. Grand Rapids: Wm. B. Eerdmans, 1989.

Richardson, Jan L. *In Wisdom's Path: Discovering the Sacred in Every Season*. Cleveland: Pilgrim Press, 2000.

Robinson, Anthony B. *Transforming Congregational Culture*. Grand Rapids: Wm. B. Eerdmans, 2003.

Rosenberger, Dale. *Who Are You to Say? Establishing Pastoral Authority in Matters of Faith*. Grand Rapids: Brazos Press, 2005.

Smith, Huston. *The Soul of Christianity: Restoring the Great Tradition*. San Francisco: HarperSanFrancisco, 2005.

———. *Why Religion Matters: The Fate of the Human Spirit in an Age of Disbelief*. San Francisco: HarperSanFrancisco, 2001.

———. *The World's Religions*. San Francisco: HarperSanFrancisco, 1991.

Teasdale, Wayne. *The Mystic Heart: Discovering a Universal Spirituality in the World's Religions*. Novato, CA: New World Library, 1999.

Tolle, Eckhart. *A New Earth: Awakening to Your Life's Purpose*. New York: Penguin Group (USA), Inc. 2005.

Vennard, Jane E. *A Praying Congregation: The Art of Teaching Spiritual Practice*. Herndon, VA: The Alban Institute, 2005.

Weston, Walter. *How Prayer Heals*. Charlottesville, VA: Hampton Roads Publishing, Co., 1998.

Wilber, Ken. *The Essential Ken Wilber: An Introductory Reader*. Boston: Shambhala Publications, Inc., 1998.

Notes

Call to Worship

1. Jan L. Richardson, In *Wisdom's Path: Discovering the Sacred in Every Season* (Cleveland: Pilgrim Press, 2000), xii.

My Assumptions about Worship

1. Martin B. Copenhaver, Anthony B. Robinson, and William H. Willimon, *Good News in Exile: Three Pastors Offer a Hopeful Vision for the Church* (Grand Rapids: Wm. B. Eerdmans, 1999), 94.

2. James F. White, "A Protestant Worship Manifesto," The Christian Century (January 27, 1982), www.religion-online.org/showarticle.asp?title=1278.

Practice #1: Lead Worship from a Place of Deep Prayer

1. Bernard Bangley, ed., *Radiance: A Spiritual Memoir of Evelyn Underhill* (Orleans, MA: Paraclete Press, 2004), 140.

2. Peter Roche de Coppens, *Divine Light and Fire: Experiencing Esoteric Christianity* (Rockport, MA: Element, 1992), 120.

3. Beatrice Bruteau, *Radical Optimism: Practical Spirituality in an Uncertain World* (Boulder: Sentient Publications, 2002), 77–78.

4. Cynthia Bourgeault, *Centering Prayer and Inner Awakening* (Cambridge: Cowley Publications, 2004), 102.

5. Ibid., 9.

Practice #2: Consider What Happens to the Energy

1. Judith Orloff, *Positive Energy* (New York: Random House, 2004), 103.

2. John Bell, "O God, My God," The Iona Community (1988).

Practice #3: Move People out of Their Heads

1. Eugene H. Peterson, *The Contemplative Pastor: Returning to the Art of Spiritual Direction* (Grand Rapids: Wm. B. Eerdmans, 1989), 93.

2. Ken Wilber, *The Essential Ken Wilber: An Introductory Reader* (Boston: Shambhala, 1998), 140–143.

3. Quoted in Christopher M. Bache, *Dark Night, Early Dawn* (Albany: State University of New York Press, 2000), 5.

4. Eugene H. Peterson, "Psalm 40:7," *The Message: The Bible in Contemporary Language* (Colorado Springs: NavPress, 2002), 962.

Practice #4: Read Scripture So Nobody's Bored

1. Marva J. Dawn, *Reaching Out without Dumbing Down: A Theology of Worship for the Turn of the Century Culture* (Grand Rapids: Wm. B. Eerdmans, 1995), 64.

2. Jacques Berthier, "Stay with Me," *Songs from Taizé* (Taizé France: Ateliers et Presses de Taizé, 1999), #3.

3. Marty Haugen, "Bring Forth the Kingdom," (Chicago: GIA Publications, Inc., 1986).

4. William Kethe, "All People That on Earth Do Dwell," Tune: Old Hundredth; Text: L.M.; Based on Psalm 100, 1561.

5. Miriam Therese Winter, "My Soul Gives Glory to My God," *The New Century Hymnal* (Cleveland: The Pilgrim Press, 1995), #119.

6. "What Wondrous Love Is This," Tune: Wondrous Love.

Practice #5: Make Every Part Match

1. Thomas G. Long, *Beyond the Worship Wars: Building Vital and Faithful Worship* (Herndon, VA: The Alban Institute, 2001), 21.

Practice #6: Use Fewer Words

1. Maggie Ross, "Liturgy in Truth: Transfiguring the Mind and the Heart," *Weavings: A Journal of the Christian Spiritual Life* 21, no. 3 (May/June 2006): 33. Used by permission.

2. Daniel Ladinsky, *Love Poems from God: Twelve Sacred Voices from the East and West* (New York: Penguin Putnam Inc., 2002). Used by permission.

3. Thomas G. Long, *Beyond the Worship Wars: Building Vital and Faithful Worship* (Herndon, VA: The Alban Institute, 2001), 92.

4. C. S. Lewis, *The Lion, the Witch and the Wardrobe* (New York: Macmillan Publishing, 1950), 75–76.

Practice #7: Create a Safe Intimacy

1. Coleman Barks, trans., *The Essential Rumi* (San Francisco: HarperCollins, 1995), 188.

2. Dale Rosenberger, *Who Are You to Say? Establishing Pastoral Authority in Matters of Faith* (Grand Rapids: Brazos Press, 2005), 20.

Practice #8: Make Worship Inclusive

1. Jean Vanier, *From Brokenness to Community* (Mahwah, NJ: Paulist Press, 1992), 16.

2. Marjorie J. Thompson, *Soul Feast: An Invitation to the Christian Spiritual Life* (Louisville, KY: Westminster John Knox Press, 1995), 122.

3. Eknath Easwaran, *Badshah Khan: A Man to Match His Mountains* (Tomales, CA: Nilgiri Press, 1999).

4. The Lord's Prayer: English translation of Maori language, *A New Zealand Prayer Book* (Auckland, NZ: William Collins Publishers, 1989), 181.

5. Maren C. Tirabassi and Kathy Eddy Wonson, *Gifts of Many Cultures* (Cleveland: United Church Press, 1995), 24. Reprinted from *With All God's People: The New Ecumenical Prayer Cycle: Orders of Service,* compiled by John Carden (Geneva: WCC Publications, 1989).

6. The Taizé Community in Taizé, France, is an international, ecumenical monastic community of Protestant, Roman Catholic, and Eastern Orthodox monks founded in the 1940s by Brother Roger Schutz. It is known for the beauty of its chanted prayer and its worldwide ministry to youth.

7. The Peters Projection World Map attempts to minimize the distortions favoring the Western industrialized world that are present in more traditional maps. Information accompanying the map explains those distortions. Viewing this map leads to excellent discussions. It is available at www.amazon.com, www.ODT.org, or 1-800-736-1293.

8. Walter Wink, *Engaging the Powers: Discernment and Resistance in a World of Domination* (Minneapolis: Fortress Press, 1992), 319.

9. Dale Rosenberger, *Who Are You to Say? Establishing Pastoral Authority in Matters of Faith* (Grand Rapids: Brazos Press, 2005), 107–108.

Practice #9: Integrate Music More Fully

1. John Bell, "Sing a New Song," *The Christian Century* (July 25, 2006): 20–23.

2. The Taizé Community: See Practice #8, note 6.

3. Ken Medema, "Moses," (Nashville: Word Music, 1973).

4. Mark B. Sanders and Tia Sillers, "I Hope You Dance," (Milwaukee: Hal Leonard Corporation, 2000).

5. John L. Bell, "Sing Hey for the Carpenter," The Iona Community (Chicago: GIA Publications, Inc., agent, 1987).

Practice #10: Insist on Integrity in the Worship Service

1. Cynthia Bourgeault, *Mystical Hope: Trusting in the Mercy of God* (Cambridge: Cowley Publications, 2001), 98.

2. Walter Wink, *The Powers That Be: Theology for a New Millennium* (New York: Doubleday, 1998), 42.

3. J. Gelineau, The Taizé Community, *Songs from Taizé* (Taizé France: Ateliers et Presses de Taizé, 1999), #4.

4. Jacques Berthier, The Taizé Community, Songs from Taizé (Taizé, France: Ateliers et Presses de Taizé, 1999), #10.

5. Julian of Norwich, *Enfolded in Love: Daily Readings with Julian of Norwich* (New York: Seabury Press, 1981), 36. Copyright by Darton, Longman and Todd, Ltd., London.

Benediction

1. Henri Nouwen, *The Wounded Healer: Ministry in Contemporary Society* (New York: Bantam Doubleday Dell Publishing, 1972), xvi.